W9-BWY-766

GLADLY LEARN

Leadership: Learning, Teaching, and Practicing

GLADLY LEARN

Leadership: Learning, Teaching, and Practicing

Ballard Morton

Crescent Hill Books

ISBN 1-889937-08-8

Library of Congress Catalog Number 97-69474

Printed in USA

Crescent Hill Books
2843 Brownsboro Road
Louisville, Kentucky 40206
502-899-5827
502-896-9594 fax
Order line 1-800-224-6708

Acknowledgments

My special thanks to:

All my students who have truly been my teacher. They have taught me that a teacher needs students more than students need a teacher.

All the executives who have participated in the Effective Executive programs. They have helped me learn about leadership.

All my colleagues at the College of Business and Public Administration at the University of Louisville for their support and acceptance of me as one of their own, and especially those colleagues who have participated in my special programs on self-development.

Mary Ann Forsee who taught me about computers.

Warren Lewis for his superb editorial advice.

Dick Spangler for his suggestions, support, and especially his friendship.

Bob Taylor for his support, for giving me the sabbatical in which to write the book, for bringing to life my *cacöethes scribendi*, and for giving me such superb guidance and editing help.

My daughter, Mimi, for her helpful suggestions and sharp editorial eye.

And my heartfelt thanks to my wife, Muff, whose tough love makes her a fine editor and critic. She is the only person in the world who can tell me I'm wrong and make me feel good about it. Truly she is "my sun, my moon, and all my stars."

Table of Contents

A CLERK ther was of Oxenford also...
Of studie took he moost cure and moost heede.
Noght o word spak he moore than was neede,
And that was seid in forme and reverence,
And short and quyk and ful of heigh sentence.
Sownynge in moral vertu was his speche,
And gladly wolde he lerne and gladly teche.

—Geoffrey Chaucer

Foreword

The business schools in our universities are populated with professors who for the most part "have never met a payroll." On the other side of the fence, our business managers have never faced classes of students who come from heaven knows where, laden down with undiscovered strengths and untested judgements. That gulf between good professors and good managers is an unfortunate divide because both groups have much to offer each other as well as much experience and knowledge to discuss with eager students.

Ballard Morton, in his life and in this book, bridges that divide.

Mr. Morton has been a businessman—a very successful one who has decades of practical experiences as a corporate executive and as a director of several major corporations. His directorships have covered the fields of finance, media and retailing, not to speak of numerous charitable institutions.

When offered an opportunity to teach in the University of Louisville as an "Executive in Residence," he accepted with some certainty because "he had been there, done that." Much to his surprise, his students, by their responses and their failure to respond, taught him; and he learned, as his book's title, a quote from Chaucer, indicates.

This book is about students and how they learn. It is also about a professor and how he became a better teacher. It is a success story that will benefit other executives and other professors who are open to new or different approaches to communication with their fellow board members or with eager students, as the case may be.

Mr. Morton has chosen to teach an elusive trait: leadership. We all have seen leadership in action, some yielding good results and, unfortunately, some yielding pain and disaster. This book investigates what good leadership is: integrity. It dissects leadership and discovers truths—perceived, yet forgotten—which make differences in our lives, such as listening to understand as opposed to listening to respond.

Since Mr. Morton has been my friend for over 50 years and my backpacking companion over a thousand miles of Rocky Mountain wilderness trails, I have seen this book coming. When it arrived, I wanted to have this honor of writing the foreword. My own fortunate business experiences, as well as my opportunity for the last 11 years to be president of a major university, have placed me in a position to see the value of this book. Reading it has helped me, and I believe it can help you.

—*C.D. Spangler, Jr.*
President, The University of North Carolina
Chapel Hill, N.C.
May, 1997

Introduction

I have been involved in leadership all my adult life. For thirty years I have been on the boards of directors of large business organizations, for sixteen years I was CEO of a broadcasting company, and for the last thirteen years I have been teaching "leadership" to MBA students and business executives.

This book tells about what I have learned about leadership and how I learned it. It is the story of my transition from a position of leadership in business to teaching in the classroom. I want to share what I have learned in the boardroom and the classroom in the hope of providing insights and ideas for readers who want to become more effective as leaders. To be an effective leader, I think you have to become an effective teacher. No matter whether you are teaching students or fellow executives, the way you interact with them will determine your effectiveness. I want to help the reader learn from what I have learned. This is the story of my journey—a journey of discovering more about learning, teaching and leading—and most of all, a journey of discovering myself.

In 1959, at the age of 27, I became a general partner in the Louisville investment firm, J.J.B. Hilliard & Son. This was a splendid opportunity for me to learn about leadership. In those days all investment firms were organized as partnerships. Most partnerships were not well-managed. The partners were there to sell—to bring in the money. I did not enjoy selling, but became increasingly intrigued with management. Fortunately my partners were supportive and allowed me to concentrate more on the management side of the business. I especially enjoyed working with the branch managers. By helping each branch manager to develop and increase his productivity I was able to make a greater contribution to the firm than if I had just concentrated on my own sales production.

In 1964 fate stepped in. Tragedy struck the family of my aunt, Jane Morton Norton. Her husband, George Norton, was killed in an automobile accident in February, 1964. He had founded WAVE, Inc., a broadcasting company which started the first television station in Kentucky. It now had several radio and television stations and extensive real estate holdings. Jane had inherited the entire company. Then in May, 1964, her son—who had become president of the company—was killed in an accident. I was close to Jane and the Norton family—her son was my best friend—and she asked me to join the company and help run the operations and help settle the estate.

At the time I was 32 years old. It was an extraordinary opportunity for me to learn about and practice leadership. Working at Orion Broadcasting (the name was changed) was a privilege for me. For sixteen years I was CEO, and Ralph Jackson was my close associate and confidant. We worked well together. I learned a lot from him, and I couldn't have had a finer person to work with. He is one of the best managers I have ever known, and we developed a relationship of mutual trust and respect.

My position at Orion gave me opportunities outside the company as well. I quickly became more actively involved in the broader Louisville community serving on the boards of several not-for-profit organizations. I was also elected to several corporate boards at a young age. This exposure gave me the opportunity to learn about corporate governance and leadership from people who were much older and more experienced than I was.

We sold Orion in the early 80s, and after the new owners settled in I needed to move on. I was looking around for something new when I got a call from Dean Peters at the University of Louisville School of Business. He mentioned "executive in residence." It sounded good—it had a nice resonance to it—and it sounded interesting. We met for lunch and he explained that several business schools had executive-in-residence programs. He was thinking about a one-year appointment with my main mission to build a bridge between the business school and the business community in Louisville. I could concentrate on administration, I could do research, or I could teach if I wanted to. That caught my attention.

In October 1983, I officially became the Executive in Residence at the School of Business at the University of Louisville, and in January, 1984, I started teaching my first class— "The Manager: A Practical Approach."

This class evolved into two courses: (1) "Leadership," a course that I now teach to graduate students getting their MBA degrees; and (2) the Effective Executive program, a course for senior executives in both business and not-for-profit organizations that I teach jointly with Bob Taylor, dean of the College of Business and Public Administration at U of L.

My students are adults. Nearly all of them work full-time, many are already in management positions, and many are married and have children. I treat the students the same way I treat the executives: we are trying to learn how to become more effective leaders by becoming more effective in our dealings with others and more effective in contributing to our organizations. This book tells the story of what I do in the classroom, what I have learned, and how I learned it. My teaching has been influenced by what I learned from practicing leadership, and my thinking on leadership has been influenced by what I learned from my teaching.

What do I know about leadership? How have I learned it? I have discovered that when it comes to leadership I am a slow learner. When I first started teaching I thought I knew so much about leadership—after all, I had been practicing it for 25 years in the business world—that I could just impart my knowledge to the students. I could teach them what I knew, and I would help them to become more effective leaders or managers. It didn't work out that way.

I really did not start to learn about leadership until I started learning about myself and started learning from my students. This book tells my story, my transition from a posisiton of leadership in business to teaching in the classroom. *How* I have learned has been as important as *what* I have learned. I want to share both the how and the what in the hope that you, the reader, will gain insights. My emphasis is on leadership, but I am ultimately talking about effectiveness— in your work and in your everyday living.

1.

Boardroom vs. Classroom

Altogether I estimate I have attended about 1,400 board meetings, including those of my own company. Since I have been teaching I estimate I have taught some 700 classes. It occurs to me that not too many people have had as much experience as I have had in both the boardroom and the classroom.

I was in my 20s when I first joined the board of directors of a corporation. It was a small, privately-held company, The Louisville Varnish Company, and I was asked by a friend to represent his family's minority interest. It was not a pleasant experience. All the other directors were insiders, and the CEO made it clear that I was not welcome. In fact, he refused to pay me a director's fee, maintaining that I was providing no value to the company. It was not hard for me to determine that I never wanted to represent a minority shareholder again.

From that inauspicious beginning I was elected to other corporate boards in my early 30s. I was 32 years old when I joined the board of Citizens Fidelity Bank (later PNC Bank, Kentucky), 34 when joining Louisville Gas and Electric, and 35 when joining Kroger. I am still on the boards of these companies, nearly three decades later. (I retired from the PNC Bank board in February, 1997.) That is an unusually long association. In the meantime I have served on some half-dozen other corporate boards. What have I learned from this experience?

I have concluded that there are a number of similarities between the boardroom and the classroom. The chairman sets the tone for the meeting, just as the teacher sets the tone for the class. Is it a lecture format or a discussion format? How much control does the chairman/teacher exercise? How are the participants treated? What information is presented and how is it presented? Who presents it? How is technology used? Is participation encouraged? Are discussions controlled or free-flowing? How focused is the session?

The major similarity, of course, is the role of the chairman and the role of the teacher. A good chairman and a good teacher create an environment where maximum learning takes place. That should be the objective, but both the chairman and the teacher often lose sight of that objective.

It seems to me that a good chairman should get the greatest possible contribution from each board member and from the board as a whole. You obviously can't do this all the time, but over time this is an ideal to pursue. To do this the chairman must create a climate where board members are encouraged to share their knowledge and experience, where they are urged to participate, and where their questions are sought and welcomed. If the agenda is too detailed, long, routine, or formal this won't happen. If the meeting is taken up with the chairman, or someone else, making all kinds of slick presentations with fancy graphics, it won't happen. You can substitute teacher for chairman, and the same thing applies to a class.

A good chairman, like a good teacher, must learn to

listen. When we first think of conducting a meeting or teaching a class, we think of speaking. At least I did. Obviously you have to do a lot of speaking. But to get the best results you also have to learn to listen to the others in the meeting. You have to draw them out and get them to participate and voice their opinions. And how you respond to them will determine whether any real learning takes place.

It's a matter of control. Most chairmen want total control of a meeting. Most teachers want total control of a class. In this circumstance, little learning takes place. Information might be given out, but there are no connections, no synergy. A chairman has an extraordinary opportunity at every meeting. The experience, knowledge, and talent around the table are so often kept dormant. If the chairman can tap into this exceptional resource, boards would be more effective, chairmen would be more effective, and the companies would be better served.

I have had to learn to give up the tight control I used to exercise in the classroom. I have had to pare down my agenda and allow more time for students to discuss what is on their agenda. I had to learn that effective communication means dealing with people where they are, not where I am. I am not suggesting that all board meetings could be run like a good class. The purpose is different, the legal issues are different, and the required actions are different. But in terms of a communications process, they are not all that different, and those chairmen who recognize this are the most effective.

A phenomenon that I have observed in many CEOs is almost a paranoia about their subordinates' presentations to the board. They seem to demand a slick presentation, documented and illustrated with lots of facts. They don't tolerate slip-ups or mistakes, and they don't want their subordinates to go over the time limits set in the agenda. A slick, fast-paced, hard-punching presentation is what they want. Above all, it should be *professional*, whatever that means.

The funny thing about this is that when those same CEOs are on the receiving end of these kinds of presentations in other board meetings (where they are members of the board and not the CEO), they don't listen to them. They take in the points quickly and then tune out. They tune in when the speaker connects with them in a personal, emotional way, usually through a story or anecdote.

I think presentations would be more effective in most situations in the board meeting if the CEO would relax and let others make their presentations in a more natural, conversational manner, making sure they connect with the directors through relevant stories, anecdotes, and illustrations. This method would not work for all presentations, but it certainly would improve the routine ones. It would take a lot of pressure off managers who become a nervous wreck because of the attitude of the CEO. These managers could just be themselves and communicate in their own natural style. They would not feel compelled to *read* their presentations and be so stiff and formal. They need to be organized and know precisely what their point is, but they could just talk and tell the board what is going on—in a way that the board would get a clear picture and feel comfortable in interacting with them. I do think, however, that time limits must be insisted upon.

My chief complaint about many board meetings is that too much time is spent on reiterating numbers. I see no reason for the chief financial officer, or his or her representative, to go over lists of numbers that appear on a graphic or chart. We can read the numbers. What we need is help in interpreting them. What are the stories behind the numbers? What is management doing to improve unfavorable results? Too many operating people give too much operating detail. It goes in one ear and out the other.

A good financial report should help directors get a clear picture of what is happening in the organization. I think a CEO should prepare an agenda by asking, "How do I help the directors learn about this company, and how do I help them increase their understanding?" The CEO should also ask, "How can I learn from my directors, and how can I conduct the meeting so that the greatest learning will take place—both for me and for the directors?"

I think that some CEOs create a climate of fear for their subordinates who make presentations to the board. This climate is not conducive to effective communication. Presenters should be allowed to communicate in their natural style. They should not be forced to be some formal automaton who makes no mistakes but adds no life. They should bring their own experience and knowledge into the presentation so that they can help the board members understand their message.

No one enjoys watching or listening to someone who is uptight and a nervous wreck. The purpose is not a slick presentation or perfection. It is to help the directors gain insight and understanding. I do think that presenters must strictly adhere to the agreed-upon time limits in their presentations. But there should always be time for directors' questions. If the agenda gets behind because of directors' questions, the CEO should feel that he or she is running a good meeting.

Personal Board Experiences

When I first went on the Citizens Fidelity Bank board, we had *weekly* board meetings. The entire board approved all the loans above a minimal amount. Needless to say, the board meetings were highly routine, focusing on details, actually trying to find mistakes. We were so immersed in details that we had little time for focusing on the bank's strategic performance. It was a clubby atmosphere where the directors treated the officers as clerks.

This environment changed over time with stronger CEOs. Under David Grissom the board meetings became more meaningful. David insisted on devoting time to discussing issues that boards should be addressing, and he was good in getting directors who had had pertinent experience to share their views. The current CEO, Mike Harreld, does a good job of following in this tradition, although the role of a subsidiary board in a large bank holding company is somewhat nebulous at present.

Jim Davis was chairman of Porter Paint, and I was on that board for about 15 years until the company was sold in 1987. We had quarterly meetings, and directors were geographically dispersed. At the end of each meeting, Jim would go around the room and ask each director to give his view of business conditions and outlook. It took only 15 or 20 minutes and became a fascinating source of information for all of us. It was a great idea that can be used for a small (in number) board.

When I first went on the Louisville Gas and Electric board I was associating with men not my father's age, but my grandfather's age. The industry, the culture, and the time all called for the meetings to be extremely routine. Everything was in order and done in order. Seldom did anyone ask a question or offer an opinion. Management recommended and the board approved. All capital expenditures were carefully monitored and approved. Each resolution declaring a dividend was duly read in its entirety. You can imagine the shock when, one day, I moved approval of a routine resolution before it had been read to the board. The chairman was delighted, and from then on he did not have to laboriously read each routine resolution.

When Roger Hale became CEO of LG&E in 1989, the board meetings changed dramatically. I joke that I used to have trouble keeping awake in the meetings, and now I have trouble keeping up. Roger has assembled the finest team of executives I have ever worked with, and it is stimulating to interact with them at the board meetings.

There is no doubt that Roger controls his board meetings. He is a stickler for precise presentations from his colleagues. But I feel that he has eased up on his control of the agenda. He has recognized the benefit of the board meeting becoming a two-way communications process. We now have much more of the meeting conducted in executive session, where there are no holds barred, with open, free-flowing discussion among all the directors. Roger solicits the directors' questions and welcomes their challenges. Ultimately, I think, the company and its shareholders are better served. The strategy is more carefully thought through and everyone focuses on the important results. It is exciting being part of a dynamic organization dramatically moving to meet the challenges of the future.

The Kroger experience has been particularly rewarding for me. I have learned a great deal from a superb group of fellow directors and company officers. The CEOs, Lyle Everingham and his successor Joe Pichler, both have had a splendid ability to respect the views of each director. They have shown this respect by carefully listening. When you are listened to with respect, you are usually more careful about what you say and you are usually more careful to give your honest opinion, and not an opinion that you think would be more politically acceptable. The result is always a more honest, meaningful discussion.

Every Kroger meeting now starts in executive session. No one else is in the room, and each director feels free to express whatever is on his or her mind. The CEO, in effect, gives up the control of the agenda for this period to the board. Lyle started this practice at the time of the corporate restructuring in 1988. Kroger became highly leveraged with an enormous debt, and its approach to operating its business changed drastically. Lyle wanted to make sure that the directors felt free to question anything they wanted to. He did this at the beginning of the meeting when everyone was fresh. Each board member could now become an active participant. We became responsible for our own learning. If we didn't understand something, then we should question it. This openness and mutual respect created an atmosphere of trust, and in this atmosphere each board member has been able to make a greater contribution.

This atmosphere of openness and trust has continued under Joe Pichler. Joe is a first-rate CEO, combining the utmost in integrity with a keen intellect and an extraordinary sensitivity to the feelings of others. He is tough-minded, but a deeply caring human being. He readily gives credit to others, and he listens to them. On top of it all, he has a fine sense of humor. The result is that board meetings are enjoyable and productive. The Kroger board is a collegial group at its best, and I feel privileged to be a part of it.

Perhaps my most memorable experience as a board member occurred several years ago at Kroger. We were called to a special board meeting in Cincinnati on a Sunday afternoon. Directors flew in from all over the country. The meeting was to consider a major acquisition that would ultimately change the nature of the company. It appeared to be a done deal. The CEO of the organization to be acquired was at the meeting and made a presentation. The New York lawyers and investment bankers did all their stuff. They could taste the fees. The steamroller was moving.

After all the presentations, we finally met in executive session. On paper the transaction looked good. But there were a number of issues that didn't "feel" right to several board members. We had a frank discussion, with some directors expressing reservations, but with no one saying he or she would vote against the deal if management thought it was the best thing to do.

I'll never forget it. Lyle stepped in and said, "I can see too many of you feel uneasy about this transaction. I would not feel comfortable doing it under those circumstances. I believe too strongly in the wisdom of the board. We won't do it." And he called it off. Right there. He refused to place his ego above the collective judgment of the board. It was a remarkable performance by a remarkable man. Incidentally, to this day, those of us associated with Kroger—and especially Lyle and Joe—feel we made the right decision.

I have always subscribed to the old saw, "Experience is the best teacher." But when I honestly think about it, I'm not so sure. Experience may be a great teacher, but I don't think we learn from experience as much as we think we do. If we really learned from our experience, then we wouldn't keep on making the same mistakes. Even with 30 years of experience in the boardroom, I often don't ask the right question or focus on the right issue. I see boards and CEOs make the same mistakes they made ten years ago, but I don't do anything about it, or don't recognize it until after the fact. Somehow I need to let that great teacher—experience—help me learn to be more effective.

What have I learned from the combination of the boardroom and the classroom? Several important lessons. The chairman/teacher must:

- Have integrity.
- Create an atmosphere of trust.
- Be competent.
- Respect every participant.
- Communicate clearly.
- Listen carefully.
- Know the objectives of the meeting or session.
- Have a sense of humor.

2.

Effective Director

Increasingly we see calls for reform of corporate governance and, specifically, boards of directors. Several institutional shareholders' groups, notably the retirement systems of California and New York, want more say in how the board is constituted and how it operates. These institutions seem to want a politically correct system of governance, and they urge reform even in cases where the present system is producing outstanding results for them in the marketplace.

A lot of suggestions are coming from people who have had little experience in actually governing or running a corporation. Usually you get helpful advice by talking to people close to the firing line. With that in mind, in the summer of 1995 I interviewed a dozen CEOs who were presently running a company listed on the New York Stock Exchange, or who had recently retired from doing so. These CEOs are all acquaintances of mine, and they represent diverse companies from all over the United States (see Appendix I). I asked each person, "As CEO what have you found most effective in an outside director?"

Most of the CEOs told me they had never been asked this question before, and they found it interesting. I interviewed each one either in person or by telephone. I didn't give them a form to fill out. They responded immediately— and off the top of their heads. A few stated that they could be more articulate if given more time. I wasn't interested in a carefully articulated statement. I wanted to know what immediately came to mind. Here is what I found out.

In all cases integrity is implied. All the CEOs wanted a relationship of trust with each director and for a director to be effective he or she must have unquestioned integrity.

"Experience" is the word most often used by the CEOs. Virtually every CEO either said something about experience or said that appropriate experience was a given. One CEO said, "Experience running something," and several mentioned the need to have a majority of directors who are or have been CEOs who "have been in my shoes." As one put it, "People who have been through critical situations," who can help you when you are facing, perhaps for the first time, a situation they have already been through. Their counsel and guidance in such cases are invaluable.

Because of the nature of their company, some of the CEOs have organized their board to make sure certain critical skills are represented. One has a system where the directors annually rate each other on the identified skills the company needs. This procedure gives the company an effective way of bringing to light skills needed in new directors. This company also has a limit of ten years for tenure as a director.

One CEO has organized his board differently, placing greater emphasis on the audit committee whose function it is to focus on the performance of the company and its key people and on the clarity and effectiveness of its strategy. The board is small, and all six of the outside directors make up the audit committee, which is totally independent of the CEO. This system puts more emphasis on the performance of the whole group rather than each director acting individually.

Most of the CEOs spend time individually with directors. A couple routinely meet with committee chairmen before meetings. In every case, they look to directors for the counsel they can give. One CEO particularly emphasizes individual contacts between meetings. He counts on his directors for general intelligence about what is going on outside his industry.

Nearly every CEO mentioned something about a director who had an inquisitive mind and was actively involved in the thought processes and strategic direction of the organization. They all wanted challenging questions from their directors.

While citing the need for individual independence of board members, several CEOs referred to the importance of the collective knowledge and judgment of the board. It was extremely helpful to the CEO to have the board work well as a group. One CEO specifically tries to create a "discussion atmosphere." Another pointed out that it is easier to recruit good people to serve on a board when you already have good people who work well together. Above all, they want a board of strong individuals who cannot be controlled, but who have the civility and style to work in harmony with each other.

Several CEOs were conscious of style. The director not only should have appropriate experience, but should be willing to share that experience in a helpful manner. The director should have the ability to be critical in a constructive manner and should have an empathy for people—able to relate to all managers in the organization. One CEO referred to this trait as "comportment"—the ability to ask questions in a positive way so as not to put people on the defensive. The director should also be aware of the fine line between strategic direction and meddling in management functions.

Several CEOs mentioned the importance of diversity. They did not want to have their boards consist solely of CEOs. They had found other viewpoints and experience invaluable. One specifically mentioned "true diversity, not tokenism," and said that a foreign-born director was desirable because that person could bring a different perspective and experience to the board. A CEO told me that a particularly valuable board member had been a kind of Jewish mother to him, and she had helped him see different points of view. Another CEO mentioned diversity in age and geography as being helpful to him.

I found that the CEO's approach to the board was influenced by the nature of the company. Some of the companies were fairly young and needed specialized skills and talents from their directors. Others had a longer history and were more influenced by tradition. All of the CEOs were facing changes and all of them wanted a strong board that would both challenge them and support them as they guided their companies in this changing environment.

I learned something from each person I interviewed. Each one had a different point of view and a slightly different way of expressing himself. I got a few surprises and many observations. Here are some of their comments:

- Question: What have you found most effective in an outside director?
  Answer: Irreverence.
- In the top slot, a man either grows or swells.
- You need to question strategy from the literary viewpoint as much as from the economic. You should ask, "How is the story going to end?"
- I want challenging questions and comments that make me think at a deeper level.
- Always choose someone for your board equal or superior to you in judgment and decision-making.

- You should always talk up to your board, never down to them.
- I want people on my board who have been through critical situations and who also have a moral point of view.
- We need to find an outside director who has knowledge in technology. Such a person is hard to find. Academics are not effective—they are too theoretical.
- I want a director willing to challenge my assumptions and ideas but also willing to give me enough rope to make my decisions—even if he thinks I'm wrong.
- Directors with a significant ownership position have been more helpful.
- A director should be open to asking off-the-wall questions. To do that requires strength and confidence in yourself.

3.

Effectiveness

Being effective in the boardroom, whether you are the chairman or a member of the board, requires competence, confidence, experience, and attitude. Not all effective board members would make good CEOs, and not all CEOs make good board members. But the two roles do have a lot in common with the requirements of effective leadership.

And effective leadership is what I am interested in. How do we develop people who can be more effective, not only in the boardroom, but in the workplace? Every business school, every business corporation is trying to develop people who will be more effective in organizations—in getting results by working with others. Every executive and every student I have worked with has wanted to become more effective.

Here are the areas that I think are crucially important. These have become the themes of my teaching.

• **Integrity**. You must have integrity. You must have ethical values and you must demonstrate them in your actions—by what you say and do. People must be able to trust you. An effective board operates only in a climate of trust, and I don't think there can be trust without integrity.

• **Competence**. You must have the skills and knowledge to do the job. You must know what you are talking about based on your experience. There is no substitute for experience, but experience by itself is not enough. You have to learn from your experience and learn how to communicate what you have learned to others.

• **Respect**. Leadership is a process of building relationships, and relationships are built on mutual respect. You show your respect for someone by listening to him or her because you are genuinely interested in understanding that person's point of view.

• **Communications**. The ability to listen and the ability to express yourself in a manner that other participants can readily understand. This means knowing how to make your point and making it. It means knowing how to ask the right questions, but in a way that elicits information and understanding and does not put the other person on the defensive.

• **Community**. Leadership operates in the framework of a community. You must learn how to build a community, both as a leader and as a participant. To build a community (a team), you need to develop common values, trust, respect for each other, growing relationships, and effective communications.

• **Care**. To be effective, to make a contribution, to make a difference, you must care about your organization and the people you work with. You must care about yourself and your mission. Because you care, you demand excellence of yourself and of those you work with.

• **Self-knowledge and self-confidence**. These two go together and are dependent on each other. You must have both to be effective. You need self-knowledge to know who you are and what your values are. You then need self-confidence to express yourself and your values. It takes courage to ask the "dumb" question in a board meeting, but you must have the self-confidence to do so.

This list is obviously not all-inclusive. It represents important values that don't get "taught" in school, but which we must learn if we are going to become effective leaders. These are the issues I deal with in my "Leadership" courses— both directly and indirectly. I think that by diligently concentrating in these areas, we can become more effective as leaders and participants in our organizations.

In the rest of this book I focus on what and how I teach. I invite you, the reader, to come on the journey the students and I take. It is a journey of self-discovery and a journey of learning about leadership. Through sharing this experience, I hope to help you become more effective.

4.

Welcome to Academia

I had a helpful introduction to academic life. In the course of conversations with Don Swain, President of the University of Louisville, we discussed management and leadership, and I asked him who he consulted with and confided in. He had been on the job for only a year or so and was still feeling his way.

One thing led to another and we agreed that I would become his personal management consultant for the summer. I said I'd do it gratis, but he wisely suggested a more businesslike arrangement. And so I signed my first and only personal services contract. Having a contract—and getting paid—meant that I would do the work that Don wanted me to do, when he wanted it, and it meant that he'd listen to my suggestions a bit more carefully since he was paying for my advice.

During the summer of 1983 I frequently met with Don Swain and explored areas of communications and management at the university. I had extensive interviews with most of the administrative leaders on campus, including the deans and vice presidents. It didn't take me long to figure out that running a university was quite different from running a business. It seemed that everyone had a say in all decisions, and issues were discussed and debated endlessly. Academic administration would take a lot more patience than I had. It was not for me. I liked decisive action.

As a way of fulfilling my mission as Executive in Residence—bringing the business school and the business community closer together—I organized a series of CEO-Faculty seminars. The CEOs of the major corporations in Louisville came to the business school and met for a two-hour session with the faculty. These seminars gave faculty members— particularly the younger, newer ones—an opportunity to learn more about business in Louisville and to make contacts with leaders in the business community. And, of course, participating in the seminars got the CEOs involved in the business school and made them more aware of what we were doing.

During the fall a number of the faculty invited me to give guest lectures in their classes. I was finally getting a taste of teaching, and I loved it. I thought I would be fabulous in these classes, but reality quickly set in, and to most of the students I was just another talking head. I tried to stick closely to the subject of the course—the text—and was probably pretty boring. I was trying to demonstrate to the students—and to the professor—that I could be academic. It was exhilarating when I connected with some students every now and then. But for the most part, I doubt that I added much of real value.

At the time, I wasn't so aware of my shortcomings in the classroom, and I really enjoyed being there and interacting with the students. It had become obvious to me that the real action on campus was with the students and that is where I wanted to be. No research or administration for me. Just teaching.

In the fall of 1983, Lou Grief became acting dean of the business school, and Lou and I became good friends. We frequently had lunch together and had many conversations about teaching and about students. He was a dedicated teacher, and he was dedicated to his students. Lou, along with everyone else in administration, was extremely supportive of me and was enthusiastic about my teaching a class. I could teach whatever I wanted, whatever I thought would be helpful to the students. I could determine the curriculum, the format, everything. What an opportunity. How few teachers anywhere in the world ever get such a chance. I had to make the most of it.

As I started thinking about the class, three basic themes came to the fore: stressing communications, emphasizing the practical rather than the theoretical, and focusing on the manager.

The stress on communications was a natural for me. I was an English major at Yale, loved the English language, loved to read, and was fascinated by words and language. After all, I had always wanted to be an English teacher. I thought about my own formal schooling. What kind of class had I learned the most in? Who were my most effective teachers? Why? How did they teach?

The answers were fairly obvious. The classes that I had learned the most from at Yale were small seminars where students were actively involved in discussions. We had to write a lot of short papers and often we had to present the paper to the class. Always we got individual, detailed criticism on the writing from the teacher. In some cases, we met with the teacher in his office and he would review our papers in great detail. We paid careful attention to what we were reading—to the text—and analyzed it in critical detail. In these classes there were no tests or exams—and there were no lengthy term papers. We were expected to do excellent work for every class. We had to be prepared for each session. These images of my "best" classes at Yale became the model I would build on.

I wanted to emphasize the practical because that is what the students needed. They needed to find out what worked in the business world. I didn't have much interest in theory. I liked what worked in practice. The class should be more like business than school. Each class session would be a meeting and I would be chairman. Students would have to learn how to interact with each other more effectively, because if they were to become managers they would be spending a lot of time in meetings where they would be judged by what they contributed and how well they interacted with the other participants. I also knew that if we could have good brainstorming meetings, that is good discussions, the students would learn from each other. They would learn from their own experience and from the experience of their peers.

I would focus on the manager. Being a manager was what the class would be about and why students would take it. They wanted to become successful managers and I would show them what they needed to do. After all, I had spent a number of years trying to develop managers. I had lots of experience and had made lots of mistakes. For some time I had thought about how I could help young people in their careers and help them become effective managers. I could bring some knowledge and experience to the table.

Since this was to be a class emphasizing the practical, I determined to have a number of guest speakers—men and women who were successful managers or leaders in the Louisville business community. Getting business leaders participating in the classroom would also help further my mission of bringing the business school and business community closer together. The students could learn from interacting with these guests and they could gain valuable insights that they could never find in the typical business text book.

I got a call from Kathleen Smith, Don Swain's assistant, asking me if I had thought about a classroom for my course. Obviously, I had not. Any old classroom would do—something about a good teaching environment being a simple bench, with Mark Hopkins on one end and the student on the other. All I needed was a room with a large table we could sit around. That was not the typical classroom at U of L.

Kathleen offered me the Jefferson Room, which is the meeting room for the Board of Trustees, the formal board-room in the administration building. My classes were going to be on Tuesdays from 5:15 to 8:00 p.m., and she would see that the room was set up for me each week. This turned out to be an ideal arrangement. The room created a businesslike atmosphere for the students, and being in the administration building, it would be convenient for our guest speakers to come there and find a place to park.

I simply fell into this situation. I had given practically no thought to the setting. I had felt that the setting didn't really matter. Oh, but it does. Meeting in the boardroom made a huge difference. The minute they walked in, the students realized they were in a different, special place. It was more businesslike. It certainly was not a typical classroom. It made them think that this class was different. It was special.

What was I going to call the class? Influenced by an exposure to truth in advertising, I prosaically named the course, "The Manager: A Practical Approach."

Somebody in the business school administration sent out letters inviting selected seniors (high grade point average) to participate in a special honors class that I would teach. Everyone was casual about such required details as a syllabus. Just do it—and write up something for the students by the second class session.

I was now ready to begin. Spring semester, 1984. Fifteen students had signed up for the course. We would meet from 5:15 to 8:00 p.m. on Tuesdays for fifteen weeks.

5.

First Class

The secret of education is respecting the student.
—Ralph Waldo Emerson

The students were varied in age and experience, a rather typical description of the students in all my subsequent classes. Of the fifteen, eight were women and seven men. One was African-American. Eight currently had full-time jobs, five had part-time jobs, and two were full-time students. These were not "traditional" students. They were earning their own way and they were serious about developing their careers. Some already had responsible management positions. Their ages ranged from the low twenties to the high forties. Some had traveled widely and had quite a bit of experience in life. Others had hardly been outside of Jefferson County and were inexperienced and naive. Six of them were married, and a few had children.

My intent in the class was to explore what a manager actually does and to determine the attributes of a successful manager. There would be no exams. This was not going to be a course where an exam would be helpful or meaningful. Students would not have to memorize facts or theories and spew them back to me.

Books

I intuitively knew that I did not want to use a textbook. A textbook tends to control how the subject is presented, and I wanted the control. I was determined to make the class practical and to draw on my experience as a manager. I also wanted to involve the students in the books that business managers were currently reading. The four required books were *The One Minute Manager*, *In Search of Excellence*, *Megatrends*, and *The Elements of Style*. Everyone read these and wrote papers on them. Chapters of *The Elements of Style* were assigned throughout the semester, and we carefully reviewed these chapters in class.

I selected numerous articles and other handouts that I had used with my own managers. We reviewed and discussed these articles in class. Most of the articles came from the *Harvard Business Review*.

In addition, teams of three students each were assigned a book to read. They then made a formal oral presentation of the book to the class. I thought that the students could get some practice working in a group, and some exposure to more books and ideas. The books in this group were *The Managerial Woman* by Margaret Hennig and Anne Jardim, *The Effective Executive* by Peter Drucker, *How to Master the Art of Selling* by Tom Hopkins, *How to Get Control of Your Time and Your Life* by Alan Lakein, and *Getting to Yes* by Roger Fisher and William Ury.

Grades

I knew that grades were important to students. Grades, if done with care, can be a useful tool and helpful feedback for the student. A number of students get caught up in grades as ends, and all they become interested in is getting an A. I was determined to use grades as a means, not and end, and by grading diligently with high standards, I hoped to show students where they stood and what they needed to do to improve.

I decided that two-thirds of the grade would be based on written assignments and the other third on oral presentations and responsiveness in class. From the outset, I intended to have numerous one-on-one meetings with the students and give them specific feedback so that they would know how they were doing and what they needed to do to reach a level of excellence.

In all my early evaluations by the students, both undergraduate and graduate, my lowest marks were in the area of grading. A number of students felt that I was too arbitrary, too subjective, and too inconsistent. Giving grades is a pain in the neck, and I still don't feel that I do it all that well.

Students were held accountable for doing all assignments on time. I was tough on this issue. In business, you simply could not miss a deadline. You had to get the job done every day. I also started class on time and insisted that students be there—on time. I made a big deal of this because I had been shocked at how lax most of the university was about being on time—for meetings, appointments, or classes. I had come from broadcasting, where if you missed 30 seconds you lost money. To this day it irritates me to delay starting a meeting because someone is late. I don't think it's fair to those who are there on time and ready to work.

Writing

The writing assignments were a major part of the class. I decided to limit each paper to only one page and to have the paper written in the format of a business memo to me. I am not exactly sure why I came up with these criteria, but I was certainly influenced by the (then) well-known one-page memos at Procter & Gamble.

Whatever my reasons, the basic requirements worked beautifully and I have not changed them to this day. The advantages are that limiting the memo to one page means that the writer must focus on the subject, must know the point, and must make it. It forces the writer to think clearly. The style of the memo format is informal in contrast to the stilted high school English essay or the padded verbiage of the term paper, which must be at least fifteen pages even though it could all be said in five.

The other obvious advantage of one page is it's less for me to read. I can go over each memo several times, in meticulous detail. A teacher cannot give the same kind of feedback on a longer paper. At first, some of my colleagues felt that a short paper was not a legitimate academic exercise, but I think that most of them have come around. They heard too many positive remarks from my students, they saw how the students' writing improved, and many of them now regularly assign short papers in their own classes.

I tried to make sure that each assignment had practical applications and that students could learn something from doing it that they could use on the job. The last thing I wanted was a useless academic exercise. I carefully wrote out on the flip chart exactly what I wanted in the memo. I was the boss and this was the job the students must do for me. I insisted that they do the specific job I wanted. They got no credit for doing the wrong thing, no matter how well they did it or how hard they had worked on it. This was the way business worked, and they needed to learn it.

Guests

We had seven guest speakers. I wanted a diverse selection, not only because the class was diverse, but because I wanted the students to see that there was no one right way to be a manager. I asked the guests to share their experiences and to pass along to the students what they had found helpful in their own careers. I encouraged the students to ask questions.

The guests were mostly CEOs of Louisville businesses, most of which happened to be privately owned. The businesses included advertising, investments, insurance, retailing, healthcare, and education. Two of the guests were women and one was African-American.

Education was represented by Don Swain. He subsequently came to all my classes, which the students deeply appreciated. They loved being able to sit down with the President of the University and interact with him at such a personal level. I doubt that there is another class or university where the President participated on such a regular basis—he was a guest in every one of my classes, not missing one in eleven years. Quite a record. And I am grateful to him for it.

The students enjoyed the guests and learned from them. In a couple of cases a guest influenced a student to change careers. The students readily saw that no two guests approached their careers or their work in the same way. They learned that you must develop your own management style.

From those first guests, I learned something, too. I learned that I must sit back and let the interaction between students and guest take place without my control or interference. I also learned that guests were more effective when they talked about their personal experience rather than their area of expertise. An expert in marketing, for instance, should not talk about marketing, but about himself or herself. Guests connected with the students when they revealed something of themselves, rather than representing their title or position in the organization.

Conferences

After each of the first three memos, the students were required to meet with me in my office. We went over their memos and I gave them feedback on their writing and on their performance in class. I let them know if they needed to speak up more forcefully, make their point more clearly or quickly, and above all when they made grammatical mistakes in their writing or speaking.

After the three required meetings with me the students could meet with me and review their memos each time they wanted to. I found a tendency that is probably typical. The best students kept meeting with me. The weaker ones avoided the sessions whenever they could.

One project we did in place of the weekly memo was the résumé. I had the students write a cover letter to me, enclosing their résumé, and asking me for a job interview. I would be whoever they wanted me to be. The object was to make the interview as helpful to the student as possible.

I felt comfortable doing this since I had interviewed so many potential employees at Orion. Even though I did not do the actual hiring, I did a lot of interviewing and had experience interviewing people especially for sales and management positions.

The students met with me in my office, and I tried to make it as realistic as I could. I insisted that the résumé be printed up properly and that they be dressed properly for an interview. I then gave them feedback on the letter, résumé, and interview. I also gave them a grade on the whole exercise.

Feedback

I was tough on the feedback. I tried to be honest. After all, the students needed to know these things. As I had thought about my efforts to develop managers in my business I realized that I had often not been as direct and frank as I should have been. The problem with managing in a business is that there are always several agendas. I had felt that if I corrected a subordinate's writing or speaking, that subordinate might get the wrong idea and think that all we were interested in was writing correct memos. Clearly, I had rationalized my behavior. There was no reason to hold back with students and I was not going to.

During the semester it became obvious to me that the students needed more practice in making oral reports. Further, if they were going to become effective managers, they needed to learn how to give critical appraisals of another person's work. In addition to the formal group presentations on the assigned books, I required several individual oral reports—some formal (that is, prepared ahead of time) and some spontaneous. I designated a specific student to evaluate the presenter. The evaluator had to give the presenter immediate feedback on the presentation. I urged the rest of the class to comment on both performances, and I gave both the evaluator and the presenter feedback (and grades) on their performances.

I remember telling one younger woman that she should observe the older students in the class, watch how they conducted themselves, how they spoke and dressed, and follow their examples. I specifically told her not to slouch at the table. That was not how you conducted yourself professionally at a meeting.

Several years later at a reunion of my classes, another of the younger students, who had now become a polished and sophisticated-looking banker, told a group of us, "You were hard on my ego, but great for my career."

One of the older students presented me with a dilemma. She was intelligent and had had a lot of practical experience—but not business experience. She had sons in college. She liked Shakespeare and one of her favorite poets was T. S. Eliot. The problem was that she frequently used bad grammar in her speech.

I didn't want to embarrass her in front of her peers and yet I knew I should try to help her. I talked to her about it in one of our private meetings and discovered that she simply was not aware of how she talked. As I recall, her problems were phrases such as "He don't," "I seen him," and occasionally "I ain't."

Much to my surprise, in the next class session this student said, "I'd like to tell you all something. Mr. Morton spoke to me about my incorrect grammar. Now I've been talking that way all my life. I'm sure you all thought I was pretty dumb. But I didn't realize it. Nobody ever told me. Just think about it. I've been going to school for a long time, and no teacher has cared enough to correct me. They let me go on and keep making mistakes.

"Well, Mr. Morton cared. And he has helped me. I want you to know I appreciate it and want to thank him publicly. We are all lucky to have him for a teacher."

Needless to say, I was deeply touched. It took courage for her to state this publicly. I learned a lesson from it, too. I am sometimes hesitant, even reluctant, to give honest feedback. The issue is too sensitive or I might hurt the person's feelings. I recall this incident and realize that my job is to give just such honest feedback. Nearly all students hunger for honest feedback, and they get so little of it. When I think about it, I could say the same thing about all of us—employees, managers, teachers. We need to recognize helpful feedback when we get it and we need the courage—and courtesy—

to say thank you.

I sought feedback from the students. After all they had been in the classroom a lot more than I had in recent years. I was the novice. I have one particularly vivid memory. It was during the last class. I was standing at the end of the table next to my flip chart and was soliciting feedback on the course and on my teaching. The students were giving me what I wanted to hear. "Great course." "You're a great teacher." "You have worked me hard, but I have learned a lot." "You have helped me on my job—my boss has noticed the improvement in my writing."

I was becoming more and more satisfied with myself. My head was beginning to swell. Then Mike raised his hand, leaned back in his chair and said, "Well, I'll tell you something, Mr. Morton."

The tone of his voice brought total silence to the room. Mike continued, "The more academic you try to be, the less effective you are."

I felt that I had been stabbed. It was all I could do to keep my composure. But I knew that everyone was watching my body language. I had to remain cool. I had to show that I could take criticism as well as give it.

"What do you mean, Mike?"

"We can read. We can underline or highlight Peter Drucker. What we don't have is your experience. Why don't you share that experience with us? Why don't you open up and let us know who you really are, instead of going over and over the text?"

Now Mike was a maverick. He worked for the Corps of Engineers and had a job in management even though he lacked a college degree. He did his own thing in his own way.

He loved to get my goat, which he had succeeded in doing on several occasions. But this time he had really hit home. Wham! I needed that. This was probably the best advice I have gotten since I have been teaching. And to think

I got it from a student—a mere C student, and one who often irritated me—and I got it my very first semester of teaching!

I had felt that the students did not need to know who I was. They didn't need to know much about me. We would stick close to the text, close to the written word, and practice the needed skills. This is what they needed in order to become good managers. They needed a teacher with high standards who insisted that they do things by the book.

Mike gave me a wake-up call. I have been trying to put his advice into practice in all my teaching ever since. It's hard. It's much easier to hide behind the "subject," but to be effective I knew even then I would have to drop the mask. I simply had to open up and give more of myself to my students if I really wanted to be effective. Easier said than done.

Student Assessments

For the last written assignment of the semester, I had the students give an assessment of the class and of me. I asked them to tell me what was most valuable to them and to make suggestions for improvement.

Overwhelmingly they said that their greatest benefit from the course was writing. I think one reason for this is that we started from such a low base. In 1983 students did not have to write much, at least in the School of Business. I had one student tell me that he had not had to write anything in any class since freshman English. I found that disgraceful. He was a senior, just about to graduate. Not one of his classes had required papers—not even essay tests or exams, just multiple-choice and true-false tests. No wonder business people were complaining about our graduates' lack of communication skills.

Several students mentioned the reading and vocabulary exercises had been helpful to them. Only one mentioned an improvement in oral communications.

Many of them cited the practical skills they had developed and their increased knowledge of what skills a manager needs. The guest speakers were well-received, and several students said that they learned a lot from them.

Three mentioned increased self-confidence. Although I am not sure that my goal was specifically to help increase their self-confidence, I began to learn that this was a crucial aspect of my teaching.

That's the good news. Now for suggestions for improvement. In reviewing these suggestions some twelve years later, I am amazed at how sound, how helpful, and how accurate they were. But I simply did not realize it at the time. Ironically, over time, I have implemented nearly everything they suggested. I guess I had to think it was my idea before I could really make the change. But the truth is, those first students gave me extraordinarily good feedback and suggestions.

Here are some of their suggestions verbatim:

- The only part of the class that I felt that did not help me at all was when you read to us from the assigned articles. This is another place where the 80/20 rule applies—I had already highlighted 80% of the passages you read.
- I have two suggestions for improvement: encourage open discussions on class readings and more formal oral presentations.
- It would be beneficial for students to get as much practice in speaking as in writing; therefore, more presentations should be assigned throughout the semester. In addition to the group presentation, each week two or three different students could present their one-page memos in front of the class.
- The past few weeks of this class were a bit like the last few chapters of *In Search of Excellence*—redundant. Nothing new was happening and the learning process stopped. There also seemed to be a negative air to the class.

As an example, last week's presentation was only criticized. There was no positive feedback from you. I'm sure there must have been some positive qualities to the presentation.

• I would suggest to you Sir, that if you would speak more of your personal experiences the class would seem less mechanical.

• Grading lacked consistency. One standard was never set.

• You say "uh" too much. Just pause and begin where you stopped. In addition to this, you should exhibit a little more energy in your speech. Life or spirit in your talks would make you dynamic since everything you have to say is interesting.

Now that is telling it like it is.

6.

First Graduate Class

It is not difficult to know a thing; what is difficult is to know how to use it.
—Han Fei Tzu (c. 250 B.C.)

In the fall of 1984, I taught my first graduate class—nineteen students pursuing their MBA degrees. Since I had not gone though a graduate program myself, I probably over-compensated. I was determined to be tough and make the students jump through hoops.

My model was a combination of my image of the Harvard Business School and the television program, "The Paper Chase." Students would have to work hard and get it right. After all, they were getting a professional degree—at least I considered it a professional degree. Many of them were business professionals—six of them were already managers.

I did not use the case method of Harvard, but I did use the philosophy of giving students excessive work and putting pressure on them to figure out how to get the job done. The problem was that this was not the Harvard Business School. Most of these students were married, nearly all had full-time jobs, and several of them had children. What they did not have was time. They were highly motivated to learn, but they simply could not spend hours and hours on this class. Nearly all of them were taking other classes, too.

Since so many of my undergraduate students were older and nontraditional, I did not find a significant difference between them and the graduate students. Consequently, I structured the class and assignments along the same lines as the undergraduate class. Only there was more reading, and obviously the discussions would be more sophisticated. I used the students as resources and had them share their experience. A "case" could well be a problem one of them was working on at the office.

Over all, I received good evaluations from the students. In their assessment of the class, they listed the weekly memos and the guest speakers as having the greatest value to their learning. The personal feedback, class discussions, and readings were high on the list.

But as in the case of my undergraduate class, the suggestions for improvement were most instructive. In retrospect, I had not thought clearly enough about who my students actually were. I had a preconceived notion in mind. What I needed to do was to respond to each student and each student's needs where they were right now. They let me know that I should cut back on the reading assignments, and especially my emphasis on selling (they read Hopkins' *How to Master the Art of Selling*).

They gave me some helpful advice on class discussions. When we were discussing an issue, I would typically go around the room and call on each person for his or her opinion or thoughts—often following up with another question. In other words, I kept control of the discussion. Several students recommended that the discussions should be more free-flowing and more open. It took me a while to put that suggestion into practice, but I know the students were right, and I now give more control of the discussions to the students. I have found that when I do this, more learning takes place because as the students become more actively involved they start formulating their own questions, stimulating their thinking and their imagination.

Several students also suggested that I assign more oral reports. I did not do as much as I had intended. They made brief (two-minute) reports of their memos and we gave feedback on the spot. Clearly, they needed—and wanted—more practice. I had put so much emphasis on the written assignments that there just was not enough time for the oral reports.

Again, because of time pressure, I chose not to have the students do group presentations. I felt that scheduling for the students would have been extremely difficult, and I rationalized that they were getting sufficient practice in group presentations in their capstone "Policy" course. Wrong!

Grades and grading were still bones of contention. Both the students and I spent too much time, energy, and bickering over grades. I was a real stickler—a hardass—and was too inflexible. Too much emphasis on grades takes away from learning. Grades are merely an indictor, a subjective form of measurement, and I don't think they are the be all and end all in indicating effectiveness in learning or teaching. They should be kept in perspective. In this class I was probably as guilty as the students for placing too much emphasis on the letter grade.

7.

From Teaching to Learning

*I'd rather learn from one bird how to sing
than teach ten thousand stars how not to dance.*
                                                    —e. e. cummings

When I started out in those first classes, my emphasis was on teaching. I wanted to be a teacher—and a good one. I saw that there were a number of similarities in teaching and in managing. I could bring what I had learned and knew about management and managing to the classroom

From the students' viewpoint, I had some advantages over other professors in the School of Business who had not had business experience. Virtually all these professors—particularly the younger ones—had jumped through the Ph.D. hoops and had all the required academic credentials. They were fluent in the latest research methodology and they were publishing articles in academic journals. They knew theory, but many of them had little practical business experience in management. In many cases, the students had more practical experience than the professor, but in academic terms, the professor had more "knowledge" and knew more theory.

I have never been particularly interested in theory or research. The Ph.D. program—in business—strikes me as byzantine and bizarre. It is not designed to help students learn what they need to know to become more effective in business. Now I was hardly in a position to take on the entire business school curriculum. What I could do was to create a course that was useful and helpful to students in their careers. So I made a big point of focusing on the practical—what works in practice. I determined to call on my experience and the experience of my students.

In those first classes I created a structure that was sound. The weekly memo, class discussion, oral reports, guests, and individual conferences are still the foundation of the class. The current syllabus does not look that much different from the one in, say, 1987. What has changed the most is me. My attitude, my approach.

A student in my first undergraduate class went on into graduate school to get her MBA. Four years after that first class, she again enrolled in my class—this time in the graduate program.

When she took the undergraduate class she had been working in an agency of the federal government for about ten years. Largely because of her experience in bureaucracy, she had become bitter and negative. I was tough on her—extremely demanding. I recognized that she had real ability and the potential to do whatever she wanted. The problem was that she herself did not know how good she could be and she was afraid to take any risks.

I pushed her hard and helped her change her career, getting a position in an advertising agency. She thrived and grew in her new environment and then went on to a marketing position with KFC. She had stayed in touch with me and had called on me periodically for advice. She asked me if I thought the class would be too much of a repetition for her. I told her that I did not think so since there had been a lot of changes. Besides, I knew it would be an entirely different experience for her because of the different students that would be in this class. I was beginning to realize that a great part of the students' learning comes from the interaction with their fellow students.

When I met with her at our first conference in my office, I realized that a number of things had changed in four years. I was in a new office in a new building, and the class, now called "Leadership," met right around the corner from my office in the plush boardroom in the School of Business Building. I was looking at a positive, confident, hard-driving business executive. She had certainly developed and matured in those four years.

We looked at each other and smiled. I said, "So here we are again."

"Here we are again."

"I tell you what. I'll make a deal with you."

"What's that?"

"At the end of the semester I'll give you honest feedback and let you know how I think you've changed in these past four years. Then I want you to be totally honest with me and let me know how I have changed in that time. Fair enough?"

"Okay. I'll do it!"

We had a fine class. She was a leader and did a first-rate job. In my last conference with her it was easy for me to give her an honest evaluation, because she had grown and developed and was making such a contribution in whatever situation she was in. It's fun giving such positive feedback.

I then said, "All right. Remember our agreement. How have I changed?"

She looked me right in the eye. Then she smiled warmly and slowly said, "You've mellowed!"

That's not exactly what I expected to hear. I had not thought about it that way. But I knew her words were honest. After she left I started thinking about what she meant, and I found her words pleasing. I suppose what I had been learning in those four years had caused me to mellow, to become more relaxed about things. I did not have to always control things and stick to an overcrowded agenda. I could let things happen.

How did this "mellowing" come about? Largely from my relationships with my students. As I began to listen to them more carefully, I was better able to respond to their needs. They were telling me all along what they needed, and I gradually began to hear them and change my response and behavior accordingly.

The biggest factor in this change in me came about through my desire to be a great teacher. As a matter of fact, in the first class of each semester, I would tell the students that my goal was to be the best teacher they ever had. I was totally committed to that goal.

My initial ideal of how to be a great teacher was to impart great knowledge to the students and "teach" them the techniques for putting that knowledge to use in their careers. No question about it: they got better and they learned a lot. But deep down I knew I was not doing the job I could do or should do in giving the students what they really needed— and what I was capable of giving them. I was dealing too much with surface issues and techniques. I needed to go deeper where I could make a real difference in each student's life.

The turning point for me was a gradual one. It did not come as a sudden flash of insight. What I began to realize was that I had been focusing on *teaching*. What I needed to do was to focus on *learning*. On the student's learning and on my own learning.

For me, that has made all the difference. My whole attitude and approach changed. My objective was no longer "teaching" the students. It was to help the students learn. There is quite a difference. My job now was to create an environment where students could learn and practice what they needed to know. The class became student-centered, not teacher-centered, or subject-centered.

Every assignment I gave, every exercise, every project had to meet one criterion: will it help the student learn? This attitude caused me to think through the purpose of everything we did in class. It helped give me a confident focus and allowed us to concentrate on only those things helpful to the students' learning.

A helpful reminder that I have occasionally posted by the door of my office—so that I would be sure to see it on my way to class—simply poses a question, "Why are you telling them this?" More teachers should answer that question—before they start lecturing.

Like Chaucer's Clerk, I would gladly learn and gladly teach. Chaucer and the Clerk got it right: the learning comes first. And that's what education is all about.

8.

From Management to Leadership

In my first classes I focused on the manager and management. I felt that "leadership" was too nebulous. I wanted to be practical, specific, concentrating on skills and techniques.

Then Bob Taylor came along as the new dean of the business school. Bob had done a lot of work in the field of leadership. He had taught courses in leadership at the Air Force Academy, and he had done extensive research in the field and had written several books on leadership. After he learned more about my course, he urged me to change it to "Leadership."

Bob was ahead of his time. This was 1984, and he already knew that business schools should be focusing more on leadership and less on management in their teaching and curricula. By the 1990s virtually every business school in the country is scrambling to put together some kind of program on leadership.

In the spring of 1987 I finally came around and changed the name of my course to Leadership. I would not have made the change as soon as I did without Bob's urging. But I'm sure I would have changed it eventually. I had begun to realize that I was working more and more with my students in areas of creativity, change, and self-development. These areas fall more accurately under the guise of leadership.

I still have the last word with Bob. When talking about my course to people on the outside, I say, "I call my course 'Leadership.' The reason I call it Leadership is that no one knows what leadership is, and so I can teach any damn thing I want." I can see Bob wince every time he hears this, but there is a degree of truth in it.

I learned a great lesson about effective leadership from Bob. After he had been on the job for a year or so, he asked me to get some feedback for him. He wanted an honest evaluation of his performance from the faculty and staff in the School of Business. He asked me to interview a cross section of people in different areas and levels—I should pick them. He trusted me and said that I had credibility in the school and people would be honest with me.

I was happy to take on this task. Bob was doing a fine job as Dean and was giving the school positive leadership. But there were some rough edges. He was demanding and often short and abrupt with people. He was extremely impatient and sometimes showed irritation and anger too quickly (Bob does not suffer fools gladly). Some people were just plain scared of him—he still carried vestiges of the military. Several of the faculty meetings had been disasters as Bob became angry and totally frustrated with the lack of action or progress.

My interviews were eye-opening for me. I probably interviewed about 15 people—from department heads to clerks. They were extremely reluctant to say anything negative. They beat around the bush and talked in generalities. What I discovered was a fear that if they came forth with negative criticism, it would come back to haunt them. There was little trust in the system.

I was amazed. I knew there was quite a bit of general griping about Bob's style, but I couldn't get much that was specific from the individuals I interviewed. This was my real introduction to what I call the faculty syndrome. The faculty wants the right and privilege to complain and criticize but not the individual responsibility to do something about it.

After coaxing and pulling teeth, I got some helpful information. I then thought about it and how I would relay it to Bob. The most important thing was that he had overwhelming support throughout the school. I think the reluctance to come up with negatives on the part of some was that they were afraid if he got too much negative reaction he might just say "to hell with it" and leave. They did not want that.

When I met with Bob, I made sure he realized the tremendous support he had in the school. Then I gave the specific negatives a bit of my own interpretation. I used the information I had gotten in the interviews, but I gave it some added emphasis based on my own observations. In other words, I was harder on him than the interviews justified. I told him he needed to relax more, to give more time and patience to people, to shuck the military bearing and response, and to lighten up on himself and others and let his sense of humor come into play. He especially needed to relax about faculty meetings and regard these occasions as opportunities for faculty members to air what was on their minds rather than as an arena for action.

We had a good discussion. Bob listened carefully. He appreciated my appraisal and suggestions, and he warmly thanked me.

About a month later, we were in a faculty meeting. At one point in the meeting Bob said, "As some of you know, I asked Ballard Morton to interview a cross section of the School to give me feedback on my performance. Ballard did that, and I'd like to share with you what he told me."

I thought, "Oh, shit!" I had no idea he was going public with this.

He then spelled out in detail what I had told him. Several of my colleagues looked at me and later asked, "You told him that?"

Bob said that he appreciated the feedback and that he was aware that he needed to improve in these areas. He was determined to do so, and we could judge him by his behavior.

I was surprised and stunned by Bob's performance. And I learned quite a lesson. By being so open, so straightforward and willing to be vulnerable, Bob helped to create a trust that had been lacking. Attitudes toward him began to change. It took a big man to do what he did. He exemplified the courage and openness that are so important for effective leadership. He had demonstrated that effective leaders consider their followers (sometimes called subordinates) as people they serve and they seek honest feedback from them. They do not depend on evaluations from superiors to determine the effectiveness of their performance.

Bob also closed the loop. He not only sought feedback from his "customers," he let them know he heard their concerns and suggestions and that he was acting upon them. I've tried to remember Bob's example in soliciting feedback from my students.

Effective Executive Program

In 1986 Bob and I collaborated in creating a special course for executives. We talked about what was needed and what we could do, and we just did it. The course was based on my "Leadership" course, and I took the lead in putting it together. The major difference from my course would be the use of psychological instruments to give participants feedback on their preferences and leadership style, and anonymous feedback from their subordinates.

The class would be for 10 weeks (the regular semester is 15) and limited to 16 participants. We would meet in the boardroom from 5:30 to 8:30 one night a week and serve a light meal. Our appeal was to executives at a senior level, and the typical participant has been around 40 years old with about 15 years' experience on the job.

We called the program the "Effective Executive," with the proper salute to Peter Drucker. I was still not ready to call it "Leadership." I felt there was too much drivel in the market calling itself leadership.

We still teach the Effective Executive program every fall, and it has been a marvelous learning experience for me. Since I am basically teaching the same thing as in my other classes, it has been an opportunity to learn from a more experienced and sophisticated group. These executives in many cases are on the cutting edge in their businesses. They know what is going on in the marketplace. I can pass along what I have learned from them to my students. It helps my credibility.

I discovered a difference between the executives and my students that I did not expect. Always with my students I have made a great fuss about not talking about theory. I tell them that I don't know any theory—all we will deal with is practical—what works. The students love it. They feel they get far too much theory in their other courses, and they welcome the opportunity to deal with issues they can use right now.

When I started this line with the executives, I got a different reaction. The general response was, "We've had plenty of hands-on, practical experience. What we need is a better understanding of what we are doing and what we should be doing." In other words, some theory.

Fortunately, Bob was there. He knew the theory, and he knew how to make it relevant to the executives. Through his models and examples, he helped them gain the insights they were seeking. And, of course, it was eye-opening to me. A wonderful way to learn applicable theory without having to go to graduate school.

I have learned a lot working with Bob in the classroom. He has a rare ability to observe what is going on in a class or a meeting. Most of us are too preoccupied with our own thoughts. I have tried to be a better observer, but I usually can focus on just content or process, not both. I guess I just can't walk and chew gum at the same time.

In joint teaching, you can learn so much from each other. It is so helpful to get honest feedback from someone you respect. The learning is mutual. I remember the end of the very first class we had with the executives. We were assessing the class, and Bob said, "You didn't bring it to closure."

I said, "I didn't intend to."

"What? You've got to bring it to a close."

"That's exactly what I don't want to do. I want to open up their minds and have them leave with a lot of questions to explore and things to think about. The last thing I want to do is bring the subject to closure, as if we have finished with that issue and now have the answers."

The subject of closure never came up again.

9.

Preparation

A significant factor in being effective is the ability to look ahead. You must think through what your purpose is, what you want to accomplish. Then you must prepare.

When do I prepare for a class? That is not an easy question to answer. In one respect, I've been preparing for the next class or next semester all my life. Everything I am—what I've experienced and learned—I bring to the class. The trick is to make the most of it—from the student's point of view.

After early registration begins for the next semester, I am usually on the phone talking with Allie Goatley. Allie is head of advising for the business school and is one of those jewels that every organization needs. She is always patient with me and has helped me on countless occasions. Since my classes have limited enrollments, there are usually problems about who is admitted. Allie helps me take care of these problems—always trying to be fair to the students. I don't rest easy until there is a waiting list for each class.

I joke that the only economic theory I know is the law of supply and demand. My classes are elective. Students choose to take them. I want the demand to be greater than the supply—the places available. A strong demand gives me personal affirmation. It indicates students want what I am offering. There is also a psychological factor to scarcity. When the class is harder to get into, the students seem to appreciate more the opportunity to be there. They are more motivated to take advantage of the opportunity.

Each class is limited to sixteen students. This is not a magic number, but it works quite well. With sixteen, we are small enough to have full class discussions, and we have options to break up into smaller groups. The students can get to know each other, and I can work with them individually.

How I got to a limit of sixteen shows how academia works. When I first taught the class, I had arbitrarily limited it to 25 students, wanting to keep a seminar format. I never had that many students, but I could have easily accommodated them in the room where we met in the Administration Building.

When the new School of Business building was built, it included a boardroom with a specially designed, trapezoidal table. I had already arranged to hold my classes in this room. The problem was that only sixteen people could comfortably sit around the table. I therefore put a new limit of sixteen students on the class. After this new limit had worked its way through administrative procedures, I got a call from Mike Carroll, Chair of the Department of Management (my department). Mike said that I could not arbitrarily reduce the size of a class. We had to go through channels, and he needed something in writing. "Mike," I said, "that's all the people we can fit around the table."

"Oh," he replied, "that's a good reason. I'll take care

of it." And he did. That's the last I heard of it. Sound pedagogy has some strange ways of developing.

Prior to the first class session, I receive a class roster. After I make sure the class is full, I go down the list to try to determine gender. When the number of men and women is fairly equal, it's "Bingo!" Classes always work better when the numbers are balanced. It makes no difference if it is undergraduate or graduate, whether the students are relatively young or old, married or unmarried. More learning takes place when the class is 50-50 rather than 80-20 (either men or women). I mentioned this phenomenon to Allie one day and said that I really didn't understand why. She laughed and said, "I'll explain it to you some day!"

I also take a look at the social security numbers on the class roster. A quick glance at the first digits gives me a rough idea of where the students come from. I find that greater geographical diversity usually helps a class.

Then I do something else—in August—that I have found essential in my preparation. I go backpacking for a week with some close friends, usually in the Rockies.

Twenty years ago Dick Spangler, a classmate at Woodberry Forest School in Virginia, organized a week's backpacking trip in Yellowstone National Park, with two other Woodberry classmates, Russell Robinson and John Lee, and Dick's brother-in-law, Rob Riggs. Dick and I have been going out west for a week's trek nearly every year since, usually accompanied by one or two of the other original members.

I have found that I need the annual backpacking venture. (And I know Dick does. He has been President of The University of North Carolina System for the past eleven years. The backpacking trip is one of the few times he can really get away.) Doing something different in a completely different environment has a renewing effect on me. It recharges my batteries and helps me clarify my thinking and my priorities. I come back reinvigorated, ready for the new classes and new students.

I think it is important for leaders to get away from their normal routines. They need to gain the perspective of distance, and they need to get in touch with themselves. Going off into the mountains with close friends does it for me.

So, what have I learned from these annual treks? The importance of relationships and the crucial role of civility. In the group you just do not think of being selfish; you share with the others. You become concerned for the others, because if something happens to someone else, it affects the group, and whatever affects the group affects you. If something needs to be done, you just do it. Above all, you don't complain.

The trust is absolute. You completely trust each other because you completely depend on each other. You must be responsible for doing what you say you are going to do because the others depend on you. You do more than your share; it always evens out.

I've learned to be more of a Taoist. It is no use worrying about bad weather, lack of campsites, or anything else that you can do nothing about. You need to accept what is and enjoy it. We used to have precise itineraries and we would just about kill ourselves to make the prescribed destinations each day. Now we stop when we feel like it, or camp in the same place for several days, taking pleasant day hikes, stopping to enjoy the flora, fauna, and magnificent views.

There is something about being outdoors, about being in the mountains and woods, away from machines and commercialization, that is extraordinarily renewing to the body and spirit. You become more sensitive to everything, the wind, sun, clouds, trees, rocks, running water, and especially wildflowers. Before I went backpacking, I never paid attention to wildflowers. They were just weeds growing along the road that should be mowed. I now love to look at the wildflowers, attempt to identify them, and simply enjoy the miracle of nature that they are.

For me, an appreciation of beauty has added a dimension to my life—particularly the beauty in nature. I think an appreciation of beauty—a sense of wonder and awe—is important for a leader. It gives the leader a sense of perspective and humility; after all, we are awfully small alongside a mountain or a giant sequoia, and we can't come close to creating anything so magnificent as a wildflower. And, too, a sense of beauty underlies the power of vision. A leader who is attuned to beauty is more likely, I think, to have a vision of the ideal and be able to articulate that vision for his or her followers.

Backpacking has to do with toughness—both physical and mental. It is hard work, especially for sixty-year-olds who lead sedentary lives. It's a physical challenge, and it is exhausting. But what an exhilarating accomplishment to make it to the top of the pass, or to a campsite at the end of a long day. To set a goal and to achieve it—surely this is one of the main components of leadership.

The greatest lesson I have learned from backpacking is the importance of relationships. And leadership is all about relationships. One of the best ways to learn about building relationships is through friendship. You learn from your friends. Dick and Russell have become especially good friends of mine over the years, and I have learned about the essence of leadership from them.

When the day of the first class meeting arrives, I am ready.

In the following chapters, I present the class as it is now conducted. The students and I go on a journey, and I invite you to come along. I have learned the chronological order is important to the students' learning, and so the class sessions are described in the same order as the students experience them.

10.

First Session

Nothing is interesting if you're not interested.
—Anonymous

I get to that first class a half hour early to be sure I am there before the first student arrives. I like to check out the room and make sure everything is in order. I bring a packet of hand-outs for each student.

I have always greeted each student as he or she comes into the room. I introduce myself, shake hands, and look them right in the eye, letting them know how glad I am they are in the class (and I am glad. Suppose no one showed up? I'd be out of business). I want each of them to know that he or she is special and that this is going to be a special class. Of course, the setting helps too. Comfortable leather swivel chairs, a large, polished table, and a book-lined wall are not the norm for a classroom.

This initial encounter is important. It's the first impression a student gets. I don't know why I started it; I did not give it a lot of thought. It just seemed like a polite thing to do. After all, we were going to have a close relationship for the next fifteen weeks. I should properly make the students feel comfortable and at home.

The thought "at home" brings to mind a relevant analogy I came across in *The Art of the Obvious*. Bruno Bettelheim says that a psychotherapist ought to prepare for a new patient the way you prepare for an honored guest in your home. If, say, you are expecting not friends, but friends of friends to drop by your home—and you did not know their likes and dislikes—you would do all you could to be ready for them and to make them comfortable. Only goodwill motivates you. You still make mistakes, but your readiness frees you to be alert to please, thus creating an atmosphere in which this potential friendship between you has the best chance of getting off to a good start. This is exactly my feeling and attitude in meeting those students for the first time.

In my view, the needs of the students must come first. If I truly put the students as my number one priority, then we can establish a relationship where learning can take place.

Settling In

I invite the students to take a seat and have them print their names on a card tent that they place in front of them. This helps me learn their names more quickly, helps them learn each other's name, and eventually helps our guests to know the names of their questioners. They also fill out 3 x 5 cards giving me information about themselves, including where they work, undergraduate school, phone numbers, and interests.

I give them a compilation of advice from their immediate predecessors. For the last class of the previous semester I have the students write a short paragraph of advice to students taking this class. I have found that students will listen to their fellow students more than they will to me. When their peers tell them to relax, open up their minds, not worry about grades, express their opinions, and enjoy the class, they are more receptive to these ideas than if I said them. The new students are still skeptical, however.

I then break them up into pairs and have them introduce each other to the class. When most of us are in a new situation, we usually focus on ourselves and worry about what is happening to us. This exercise helps people focus on someone else—a trait that is essential in building relationships.

After introductions, they write in one sentence what they want to get out of the class. I want them to think through why they are in the class and what their objectives are. Having to write it down helps to focus their thinking. I have each person read out loud what he or she has written. I may follow up with a question or comment to make sure I understand what the student is saying. The statements are turned in to me, and I refer to them throughout the semester to make sure I am helping the students reach their objectives. This exercise does several things. It causes the students to make a commitment; it lets students see what their fellow students are interested in; and it gives me a better idea of what motivates them and where they want to go. If a student has a misconception about the course, this exercise helps to clear it up.

Next I introduce myself to the class. I give out my one-page résumé and a copy of a profile of me that appeared in the local business paper some years ago. For some time I did not give students this article, but in giving me feedback they told me I should share it with students at the beginning of the semester. They were telling me that I should let the students know who I was. I should share more of myself with them. I have learned that if I open up about myself, the students will more likely open up about themselves. It works better if I go first. I must tell them something about me and how I do things.

I point out that I have the marvelous title of Executive in Residence. I tell them that when I first came to the university I said I didn't want tenure. Apparently this was an unusual position for someone seeking a position on the faculty. At any rate, tenure was not for me. I did not need it, I did not want it, and I did not deserve it. This might appear to be a holier-than-thou attitude on my part, but the fact is I am in a different position than my colleagues. I have not sacrificed years of schooling and years on a tenure track. Probably more important, I have some financial independence—an enviable position to be in.

So tenure is not for me. My attitude is that I have no "right" to be in the class. I have to earn the right to be there— every time. Ultimately the students will decide if I should be there. What they get from me must be of real value to them. My "tenure" is on the line in every class session.

I have found that students are not sure how to address me. Some call me "Doctor Morton," an upgrade I am not entitled to. Others call me "Professor," an epithet I love but feel a bit guilty about accepting. I ask, "How many of you have seen the movie, *Dead Poets Society*?" Most of the hands go up. "All right, you can call me 'O Captain! My Captain!'"

I refuse the request to walk on the table, but allow as how "Ballard" is fine with me, if they won't go with O Captain, my Captain. Some students are uncomfortable with such informality and prefer "Mr. Morton," and that's certainly agreeable with me. Above all, I want them to feel at ease with me. Besides, at my age, it makes me feel younger to be on a first-name basis with students.

This is the point at which I share with them that I want this to be the best class they have ever had, and I want to be the best teacher they ever had. I point out that I can't accomplish this on my own. It depends entirely on how well we work together.

Syllabus

*All authorities get nervous when learning is conducted
without a syllabus.*
　　　　　　—Neil Postman and Charles Weingartner

We then go over the syllabus (see Appendix II) in great
detail. I tell the students that I used to claim that the class was
my creation, but I really can't do that any more. It has become a mutual creation with all the students who have taken
it. They are the ones who have helped fine-tune the class.
The point that I make is that no third party, no one from administration, has said what must be taught or how it would be
taught. Just the students and me. We are totally responsible.

That means that we have no excuses for not learning
what we need to know. If the class is not effective or successful, it is our responsibility to do something about it. The buck
stops here.

We spend some time discussing the objectives that are
listed in the syllabus. I use the word "effective" quite a bit
and at this point raise the question of what "effective" is and
how it differs from "efficient." I like Peter Drucker's distinc-
tion. *Efficient* is doing things right; *effective* is doing the right
things.

My simplistic definition of effective is getting the job
done satisfactorily (up to standard) in the least time with the
least effort. I am trying to help students become more effective at whatever they do. In this class, I want them to be effective—to do excellent work, but by learning to spend less
time and effort to accomplish it. They will get no credit for
spending long hours on this course. They get credit only for
what they produce.

My objectives for the course have remained fairly constant over the years:

1. To give you a better understanding of the manager
and leader—what they do and the skills and values
they need.
2. To help you become more effective by developing
the ability to:
   a. Think critically and creatively;
   b. Communicate clearly;
   c. Interact effectively with others.
3. To improve your skills in communicating—
speaking, writing, listening, reading.
4. To give you the chance to interact with and learn
from successful leaders (managers, executives).
5. To increase your self-knowledge and self-confidence.

I have made some clarifications in the wording, and I
think it is instructive to explore those changes.

Several years ago I added "and values" to the first objective, "To give you a better understanding of the manager
and leader—what they do and the skills *and values* they need."
I realized that that we needed to explore more than just skills.
We had to deal with values. Skills without values, without a
sense of ethics, are dangerous and inimical to sound leadership.

In 1989 I added "and creatively" to the second objective, "To help you become more effective by developing the
ability to think critically *and creatively*." This change came
about directly from a guest speaker, Bill Samuels, President
of Maker's Mark. Bill is a delight. He is extremely creative,
and he is an iconoclast. It took some doing to get him to come
to the class, and after he started talking he pulled out a copy
of the syllabus. He asked, "What does this mean, to think
critically?" He continued, "Obviously, the professor doesn't
know. The key thing to learn about thinking is to learn to
think creatively."

Bill struck a nerve. I had been thinking more and more about creativity, and so I added the phrase the next semester.

The third change in the objectives came in 1992 when I added "and self-confidence" to the fifth objective, "To increase your self-knowledge *and self-confidence*." I had found that if I wanted to help students increase their effectiveness, it was not enough to have them improve their competence and gain greater self-knowledge. They must also develop a conviction about their competence, which means that they must become more self-confident.

We discuss the grading system. I ask how many of them have had a performance appraisal or evaluation at work. Almost all of them raise their hands. "Are these appraisals objective or subjective?" The overwhelming answer is that they are subjective, even though they might employ a precise numbering system. I tell them that my system is subjective too. Two-thirds of the grade is based on their written assignments on which they get a precise letter grade. The other third is based upon my evaluation of their contribution to the class. Both of these components are subjective; they are based on my evaluation and judgment. I try to give specific feedback in both areas, letting students know what they need to do to improve.

Incidentally, since I have been teaching, I have dramatically changed my approach to grading. I like to point out Walker Percy's observation, "You can get all As and still flunk life." Grades simply don't reflect a person's competence in leadership—or much else outside the classroom. Here is the area where I have "mellowed" the most. I want students to improve their skills, and the grade is only a small part of that process.

My desire now is to get everyone in the class to the A level. When I first meet with students individually, we discuss grades and their relative importance to the student. If a student is hung up on getting good grades, I tell him or her that if they get a poor grade on a memo they can rewrite it, and I will give them the benefit of the better grade. I want them to focus on clear communication, not the grade. If they do good work, the grades will take care of themselves.

Back to the class discussion—and the real surprise: "You will get no grades on any of the oral reports or other projects that we do." This is usually followed by looks of bewilderment, relief, and occasionally disbelief. I continue, "I used to give grades on oral reports and group projects, and you know what happened? People got worse! They got more uptight—were so afraid of making mistakes they wouldn't try anything new."

After a pause, I say, "Okay. If you absolutely insist on a grade, it's an A. Does anyone want to argue about it?" Laughter. "All right, you've made your talk and gotten an A. Would you be willing to meet with me in my office and go over your videotape and see if we can mutually come up with any possible suggestions for improvement?"

I've never had a student refuse that offer. And it's one of the best moves I've made. The students can focus totally on their performance and not be diverted by the worry and pressure of a grade.

This same argument does not hold true for written work. The memo is a product that the student has produced. It stands apart from the person. Technically, I grade the product, not the student, when I grade papers. The student's self-worth is not on the line. But in an oral presentation, this is not the case. That is "you" being graded. How you delivered the speech is as important as the speech itself—and really cannot be separated. Grades on oral presentations can play hell with a student's self-confidence.

"The basic goal in the course is learning—learning how to learn, learning about yourself, and learning what you need to know to lead a fulfilling life," sums up the primary purpose of the course. The focus is on learning. Increasingly I have realized that we must teach students how to learn—or more accurately—students must learn how to learn. With the changes that are taking place in business and society, you must continue learning throughout your life, or you will be left behind.

All along I have emphasized learning about yourself. I think this is an important aspect of education, but it is too often ignored in college and graduate school. It seems that we are so eager to cram more and more knowledge into students that we devise ever more specialized courses that they are required to take. The trouble is that they are so busy chasing data and memorizing stuff that they are not able to integrate what they learn into their own lives. Schooling loses its relevance. It's often just busywork. Students must come to grips with who they are so that they can determine who they want to be.

"Learning what you need to know to lead a fulfilling life" is a phrase that I added to the syllabus in 1992. I thought about it at some length before I included it. Deep down, I knew that this was what I was trying to do in the class, but I felt uncomfortable expressing it. I finally bit the bullet. I listened to what my students had been telling me and felt I should be more open about what the class was all about. After all, isn't this where education should lead us—to a more fulfilling life?

The last major point I cover in the syllabus is that there are no exams. Exams in a course like this would be useless. I think they are useless in many other types of courses, but many professors give them because they feel they "have to." Many professors also give tests and exams because they had been subjected to them when they were in school. They want revenge. They haven't thought through the real objectives of their classes and how to help students learn. Tests and exams too often involve mere memorization. Doing well on them does not help a student develop skills useful in life outside school—unless the student is going to live in a Mandarin society. To me, it is unconscionable to give multiple choice and true-false tests in graduate school. Sadly, some of us are still doing it.

Students come across "*gaudeamus igitur*." This is the first of several Latin expressions I will toss to them. I point out that I have no academic credentials, but if I throw out an occasional Latin phrase, they might think I am a learned scholar. At any rate, since there are no exams, "therefore let us rejoice." It's from a medieval students' song, often played at graduations and is a theme in Brahms's Academic Festival Overture.

A final point I make with the students about the syllabus is what is not there. There is no statement about cheating and a student's rights. I refuse to put that in the syllabus.

Several years ago an edict was issued in the School of Business that a statement about cheating should be on every syllabus. My department Chair called me into his office and said that I needed to put the statement in my syllabus. I told him I didn't want to, and he asked, "Why?"

I said that I thought it was counterproductive. It went against the atmosphere I was trying to create in the class— one of trust. I assumed the students would not cheat. Why should I even mention the subject in my syllabus? It might indicate that I did not trust them. "Besides," I said, "your definition of cheating is what I want the students to do. I want them to work together, to help each other, and to learn from each other. It would be absurd to put such a statement in my syllabus."

"Okay, okay!" he said. "Forget it. You don't have to do it." That was the last I ever heard about it.

Break

At this point it is nearly 7:00, we've been going for an hour and a half, and we take a break. In my first classes, I gave only a five-minute break. I didn't see why students needed any more time. The break was eating into my class time, and I had so much material to cover. In the class assessment at the end of the semester several students complained about such a short break; they hardly had time to get something to eat or drink. Besides, professors typically gave a minimum of fifteen-minute breaks in similarly scheduled classes.

I didn't pay much attention to these complaints until a student told me that the short breaks prevented some good conversation among the students. She said that often students would start some lively discussions on what had been taking place in the class, only to be cut off by my insistence that they come back to class. What a revolutionary idea: students could learn something beneficial from each other without me.

When we moved into the new building I had to give them more time. The boardroom is on the third floor, and the soft drink and snack machines are on the basement level. So I went to a ten-minute break. This was still inadequate, and I reluctantly went to fifteen minutes. The trouble was that it was nearly impossible to get them to reconvene on time. Students, like all meeting attendees, will stretch any break an extra five minutes.

What to do? I found an old Indian taxi horn in an antique shop. I now toot the horn about a minute before the break ends. The business school is built around an atrium, and this atrium becomes a marvelous echo chamber. I stand on the third floor balcony and blast away.

It doesn't do much good, but it makes me feel better, and I reconvene the class on time even without the stragglers. The horn has become a kind of tradition. My former students say they love to hear the horn. It tells them all is well on the third floor. At the other end of the spectrum, an undergraduate student once told me that the way he found out about the class was hearing the horn. He was curious and decided to take the class!

Ravi, one of my students from India, loved the horn. It reminded him of his youth. I had worn a hole in the bulb, and he told me how to patch it. Not only that, when his wife went back to India for a visit, he had her bring back a new bulb. He put the new bulb on for me, and now the horn is more resonant than ever.

I did have one student in her final assessment of the class state that she resented the horn. It made her feel like a high-schooler having to respond to the bell. Just goes to show you—you can't please all the people all the time.

Requirements

After I go through the syllabus, we discuss the conduct of the class. I think the more students understand why we do what we do, the more receptive they are to participating. When they are willing to get into the flow of the class, they start becoming involved in their own learning. I tell them the class is somewhat like a brainstorming session. We are looking for ideas and not trying to be judgmental. We are not trying to compete with each other but to learn from each other. They can get editing help on their memos. Any way they can learn to write better is all right with me. I am their advocate, not their adversary.

A statement I make usually raises some eyebrows. I tell them that their job is to teach me—and each other. The thought that goes through their mind is "I am paying good money to have you teach me. What are you doing?"

I point out that each person in the room has had experience that I haven't had. If they will share their experience then we can all learn more. If they can teach me, I tell them, then I guarantee that they will learn more.

We discuss the basic requirements of the class, which are essential in creating a climate where learning can take place.

There are five:

1. Honesty—Trust.
2. Respect for each other.
3. Accountability—on time.
4. Do the job you are asked to do.
5. Sense of humor.

These requirements will be meaningless if I don't live up to them myself—in all my actions and relationships with the students. Someone once asked me, "What's the hardest thing for you in teaching?" "Practicing what I preach," I replied.

Assignments

Finally we get to the outline and assignment sheet. I prefer to keep the assignments separate from the syllabus. The assignment sheet usually has assignments for the next four weeks. Students always know what the assignment is at least two weeks ahead. I like to have some flexibility in the assignments and don't like to carve them in stone at the start of the semester.

For the second class the assignment is to read *The Elements of Style*. We will discuss both the book and writing in general. Students must write a one-page paper in the form of a business memo telling me why they are getting an MBA degree. "Tell me your story. Use 'I.'" I point out that I want to get to know them. Each of them has a unique story. I want them to tell it to me. The final product should be something that only they could write.

I also ask them to write a brief paragraph listing their name, telephone numbers, e-mail address, where they work, and what they do. I compile these paragraphs and make copies for each student. That way each student has a class roster, knows who is in the class, and how to reach them. As is so often the case with a good idea, the suggestion for doing this came from a student.

Questions

By this point the students are tired of hearing me talk. I have covered a lot of material in detail. I know that many of them have questions, so I ask, "Do you have any questions?"

Silence.

Now I know most of them are curious about a number of things and probably a few of them are genuinely confused. But they are reluctant to ask questions. It might make them look foolish or something like that.

I point out that asking questions is an unappreciated leadership skill (more on that later). I want them to acquire this skill.

I break the class into groups of four or five. They are to get together and determine what questions they'd like to ask me, no holds barred. Anything about the class or me—professionally or personally. Whatever any of them are curious about. Each group selects a spokesperson to ask the question, and I call on the groups in succession until all their questions are answered.

This is a good exercise. It puts the students at ease and puts me on the spot. There are always plenty of questions. Some are challenging, whether professional or personal. I do my best to give honest answers. I must establish my credibility. Students have amazing perception. They intuitively know that bovine excrement is bull shit.

Here are some of their more challenging questions:

- What's the toughest decision you have had to make?
- What's the biggest mistake you ever made?
- What do business leaders think about the MBA degree?

- What are the most important traits of a leader?
- What is your biggest regret?
- Who do you consider a great leader? Why?

The personal questions are sometimes a bit easier to answer, but not always:

- How did you get on corporate boards at such a young age?
- Why didn't you get an MBA degree?
- Why did you go into teaching?
- What are you proudest of in your life?
- Do you have children? What do they do?
- What do you do for fun and relaxation?

HAWLEY COOKE #4
2400 LIME KILN LANE
LOUISVILLE   KY 40222

DATE: 12/16/97
MER#: 201400004015   TER#: 0001

S-A-L-E-S D-R-A-F-T

REF: 0022   BCH: 403
CD TYPE: HC
TR TYPE: PR
AMOUNT: $21.90

ACCT: 5424180079491939   EXP: 0299
AP: 418420
NAME: PAUL E   STROBLE

I AGREE TO PAY ABOVE TOTAL AMOUNT
ACCORDING TO CARD ISSUER AGREEMENT
(MERCHANT AGREEMENT IF CREDIT VOUCHER)

X_____
TOP COPY-MERCHANT BOTTOM COPY-CUSTOMER

11.

Writing

At the beginning of Session 2, the first thing I do is have the students move into different seats from last time. Most students automatically sit where they sat before. "You must sit at least three places from where you sat last week and cannot sit next to the same person as last time." In spite of the grumbling, the students are good sports. I tell them I don't want them to get into a rut. I want them to change their outlook.

Changing seats usually leads to a discussion of meetings. We talk about the phenomenon of people always sitting in the same place in meetings. Sometimes a move can change an outlook.

I give the students feedback on the class itself. From the information they have given me, I list on a flip chart such data as undergraduate colleges, majors, places of employment, and interests. They can quickly see the diversity in the class. Most telling is the list of interests. I simply list those items that they wrote on the 3 x 5 cards, and often some of the students leave this section blank. Even so, we usually come up with a list of some thirty or so different interests. I point out this extraordinary diversity that we can take advantage of. It represents lots of different experience and knowledge. We have a great opportunity to learn from each other.

I think it helps to build a sense of community when the students know more about the group as a whole.

I then cover the next assignment, which is on speaking. They must read *How to Get Your Point Across in 30 Seconds—or Less* and write a one-page executive summary of the book. My requirement here is to write a summary that gives a clear picture of the book to someone who has not read it. No interpretation or criticism—just a summary of what the author says. They are to bring three extra copies of their memo to class because they will exchange memos with three other students and give each other feedback.

In two weeks half the class will make the first oral presentation: "Make a four-to-five minute presentation to the class on any subject you are interested in and really care about. We will videotape. Bring your own video cassette." I want them to start thinking about what they are going to talk about. We will discuss it at the conference they will have with me later in the week.

We schedule the first conferences with me in my office. I put my available time on a flip chart and at the class break they set their appointment times with me (one-half hour). Those who are on a tight schedule have to be more aggressive in getting a time-slot. It works out. Since most of the students are employed, their available times are usually clustered in early morning, lunch time, and late afternoon or early evening. I do my best to accommodate them, especially those commuting from long distances.

The second class session is challenging for me. Some of the students have already been exposed to *The Elements of*

Style, by Strunk and White, and a few genuinely like the book. But most of them are not turned on by writing, or a discussion of writing. Grammar, syntax, vocabulary are not their favorite things to think about. On the other hand, I love the subject and could easily do all the talking. My challenge is to get the students involved.

I start off the discussion of *The Elements of Style* by asking if anyone has any questions about points made in the book, or if any disagree with any of the points. We are able to clarify some points. I use *The Elements of Style* as a general reference and guideline. It is designed more for literary writing than the writing called for in our class. I prefer a more informal style in memo writing.

The points I like to cover in the book are using the active voice, using concrete words rather than abstract, keeping related words together, and avoiding qualifiers. I tell the students I have two pet peeves: *very* and *utilize*. Eliminate "very" whenever possible and utilize "use." Strunk and White have a section on the use of "he" as a pronoun embracing both genders. This no longer flies in our politically correct climate. I do not get hung up on this point, but many people do. The important point is that you are always writing for your reader, and so you should use some common sense You certainly don't want to offend your reader. I think you should stay consistent. It's ridiculous to refer to "he" in one sentence and "she" in the next when you are referring to the same person.

I am not nearly the stickler for grammar and syntax that I was when I first started teaching. Clarity and tone are more important. Good grammar and syntax usually help the clarity, but sometimes at the expense of tone. You can be grammatically correct and sound pompous or arrogant, defeating the purpose of your message. I guess I have "mellowed" here.

My favorite paragraph in the book is on page 73:

> *Rather*, *very*, *little*, *pretty*—these are the leeches that infest
> the pond of prose, sucking the blood of words. The
> constant use of the adjective little (except to indicate size)
> is particularly debilitating; we should all try to do a little
> better, we should all be very watchful of this rule, for it is
> a rather important one and we are pretty sure to violate it
> now and then.

I give the students a packet of material on writing that I have assembled over the years. There is a lot of good advice out there. The trick is to make sure students recognize the essentials they must concentrate on.

I point out that every executive I have known will always read something easy to read before tackling something more difficult. Therefore, make it easy for the reader. Use familiar words, short sentences, and short paragraphs.

The principal criterion for writing in the class is clarity. I must be able to understand what the student means the first time I read it. If I have to re-read a sentence to get its meaning then it's a bad sentence, and it's the student's problem. We write to communicate to the reader. Our job is to make the reader understand what we are saying.

The only way to write clearly is to think clearly. Clear writing is clear thinking. The problem most students have with their writing is that they don't think clearly about what they want to say. They just start writing and hope that the reader will figure out what they mean.

The best method for writing memos in my class, I have found, is to think about why you are writing the memo. What have you been asked to do? When the thoughts become clear, write the memo fairly quickly. That way it is more likely to have a smooth flow. Then edit it and produce the final document. Virtually all the students now use word processors, so editing becomes much easier. In other words, one rough draft and then the final document. I don't find it effective to do several rewrites of a business memo. The real time should be spent on the thinking, not the writing.

William Zinzer says it so well in *Writing to Learn*:

> My advice to type A writers begins with one word: Think! Ask yourself, "What do I want to say?" Then try to say it. Then ask yourself, "Have I said it?" Put yourself in the reader's mind: Is your sentence absolutely clear to someone who knows nothing about the subject?
>
> If you force yourself to think clearly you will write clearly. It's as simple as that. The hard part isn't the writing; the hard part is the thinking.

I am indebted to Wendell Berry for the thought that *sentence* means literally "a way of thinking (Latin: *sententia*) and it comes from *sentire*, to feel. Effective writing requires not only clear thinking, but the ability express feelings or emotions as well. Students need to find their own "voice" in their writing, to develop their own style. I used to try to get the students to write in one certain way (like my way), but I gradually realized that was not the way to teach writing or to help them become more effective in their writing. They need to express themselves in their own words, but they must make sure the reader understands what those words mean.

I try to get the students to write in a conversational style. If they write in a flowery, literary style with lots of abstractions, they will not usually express themselves clearly, and the reader won't readily understand what they are saying. Since clear writing is clear thinking, I ask, "What do you do when you think? I believe that you have a conversation with yourself in your brain. And you use your everyday language, not abstract, literary words. So just use those words in your writing, and your meaning won't get lost in the translation into abstract words."

I thought I was original in my thoughts on having a

conversation in our brains, but then I discovered that Plato had said much the same thing in the *Sophist* more than 2,000 years ago:

> Thinking and spoken discourse are the same thing,
> except that what we call thinking is, precisely, the inward
> dialogue carried on by the mind with itself without spoken
> sound.

So much for the originality of my thinking.

I give the students a handout with five suggestions for effective writing:

1. Think clearly—about the job.
2. What are the essential points you must make to do the job?
3. Write for the reader (ear). If it doesn't sound right, it probably isn't right.
4. Is it clear? Does it give a clear picture?
5. Ask "Have I done the job?" and edit—read it slowly out loud. (It's even better to have someone else read it.)

The handout concludes with a quote from Cato the Elder, *"Rem tene verba sequentur."* He was right to the point. "Get the concept (thought, thing) right and the words will follow."

After our discussion of writing and emphasis on using simple, familiar words, I start talking about vocabulary. "Welcome to the world of paradox. Get used to it. Management is filled with paradoxes." The paradox is that even though you should not use complex, unfamiliar words in your writing, you should constantly work to increase your vocabulary, your knowledge of words and what they mean. The reason is not for your writing, although a precise use of words is essential. It is for your reading comprehension. The best way to improve your vocabulary is through reading, and reading in a variety of fields. The greater your vocabulary, the more likely you are to comprehend what you read.

I have been told by an industrial psychologist that as a classification CEOs have the largest vocabulary of any group in this country. On average CEOs have a larger vocabulary than lawyers, doctors, or journalists. When you think about it, it makes sense. These professions have a specialized vocabulary. CEOs, on the other hand, must have a broader vocabulary, since they deal with so many different constituencies. They are generally more widely read.

The psychologist told me that this is one of the reasons for giving vocabulary tests in assessing candidates for job promotions. A larger vocabulary usually indicates someone who is more widely read with more varied interests than the narrow specialist. Now obviously you don't become a CEO because you have a good vocabulary. But the lack of a good vocabulary just might keep you from becoming one.

I give the students a vocabulary test based on words used in *The Elements of Style*. I then pass around a dictionary and have each student read the correct definitions to the class. The students are amazed. Often they have no idea what the word means. Sometimes two students will have widely differing definitions, and both of them are wrong.

They get the message. Be careful of using unfamiliar words. Your reader might not know what you are talking about. We are supposed to be able to read and understand material more sophisticated than a high school text book. You can fail to understand the message when you don't know the meaning of the words.

12.

Writing Exercise

The first part of the third class session is devoted to a writing exercise that I have used since my first graduate class. Groups of students get together, exchange memos, and give each other feedback on the memos.

I got the idea for this exercise from a seminar conducted by a man who headed the Center for Writing at Harvard. He met with some faculty members at U of L and told us that one of the best ways for students to learn about writing was to meet in a group, exchange samples of their writing, and then give each other suggestions for improving. It sounded like a good idea to me, and I quickly implemented it in the graduate class I had just begun teaching.

I have done this exercise in every class since then, but with many modifications.

Students know ahead of time that they are going to do the exercise. They bring extra copies of their memo with them to class. They break up into groups of four or five and they exchange memos within the group, reading all the other memos. They talk to each other about the memos and offer any suggestions for improvement.

The memo itself is an executive summary of *How to Get Your Point Across in 30 Seconds—or Less*. I give the students these criteria, which are what I use in evaluating the memos:

1. Does the memo cover the essentials of the book?
2. Is it clear, easy to read?
3. Can someone who has not read the book easily understand the memo?
4. Has the memo been edited properly?

The purpose of the exercise is to learn more about effective writing and to learn more about giving and receiving feedback from peers.

Students almost unanimously say they like seeing the other memos. They are not so nearly unanimous about giving and receiving feedback. I point out that this activity is one they must attempt to master, because it is essential to being a good manager or leader. This is an area of weakness of most managers I have worked with, caused, I think, by their lack of training and lack of practice in giving constructive feedback or coaching.

I also point out that this is a class in leadership. They can take the lead in exchanging memos with others in the class any time they want. After all, they must take responsibility for their own learning.

13.

Speaking

If you want to lead the people, speak to their eyes.
—Napoleon

After the writing exercise, the students have a good idea of what Frank says in *How to Get Your Point Across—in 30 Seconds or Less*. The book is easy to read and to the point (it had better be, with a title like that!). The students find the book helpful, and they can immediately practice Frank's recommendations. His major point of knowing your objective helps students learn to focus both their oral and written communications.

My Emphasis

Over the years I have learned a few, essential points that help students improve their oral presentations. Here's what I emphasize:

• You must know your purpose or objective. You must be able to state your objective in a simple, declarative sentence. If you can't, you won't know what you are talking about and neither will your audience.

• Who is your audience? What do they want from you? What do you have to give them? Communications is a contact sport: you must make contact. You must connect with the audience where they are right now—not where you are. And you must do this on an emotional level. Connections are based on emotions, not facts.

• How to connect? Through stories. Personal stories, anecdotes, word pictures, illustrations, analogies, metaphors build the emotional bridge to the audience. Using this method will help the audience get your point.

• Be yourself. Be natural. Use your normal, one-on-one conversational style. Try to make eye contact with each individual in the audience; don't be thinking about talking to a group—just individuals, one at a time.

• If you must convey factual material, present it visually or in a handout. Don't read it. Don't read charts or slides. Don't read your speech. Talk to the individuals in the audience and tell them your stories.

• Expect to feel nervous at the start. We all do. Accept your nervousness as being natural and not something to fear or get upset about. Turn that nervousness into energy to connect with the audience. The audience doesn't dwell on your nervousness and neither should you.

• Be enthusiastic. You must really want to share your thoughts, knowledge, experience with the audience. In nearly every case you are asked to make a presentation, you are the expert, and the audience wants to know what you have to say.

I try to wean the students from their notes. A lot of their problems come from what they have experienced in school. They are asked to make a presentation on a subject they have little interest in, and they are judged on the content—and sometimes on the form—and they get points off for any mistakes or omissions. Under that scenario, no wonder they get nervous and no wonder they tend to read their speeches. Nobody enjoys or gets much value from such an ordeal—neither the speaker nor the listener.

Once you know what your purpose or point is, then you should select about five stories to help your audience understand your point. You don't need to give a lot of factual information. Nobody remembers it. They remember stories. Through stories you help the audience see, hear, and feel what you have experienced. They connect with you emotionally and get your point more effectively.

I often ask students if they can remember the text of a sermon they have heard. They never can. But they can remember the stories and from them get a fairly clear idea of what the sermon was about.

If you tell stories, you don't need a lot of notes. They are your stories, and so you just tell them. The only notes needed for this kind of presentation can be written on one card. Just a brief reminder of the order of your points or stories. I have found that five points are about all you can make effectively in a short, five-minute presentation. If you must make more, then you need some visuals or handouts. The listeners are getting the message for the first time. They are unfamiliar with it and cannot absorb much new data.

The beauty of telling stories is that you can just be yourself. That is also how you can be most effective. After all, what do you have to contribute? It's you. Your knowledge, your experience, your insight.

Preparation

I believe in preparation. I urge students to discover

what works best for them; there is no one right way. When I am asked to give a talk, I think about the audience and why I have been asked to talk. This process helps me focus on my objective. I determine the length of the talk and then decide the points and stories to include to make my main point.

I write an outline with a few notes. Referring to the outline and notes, I talk into a tape recorder. Then I play it back. This has been a helpful process for me. I immediately get a feel of what the audience will hear. I never like it; I am so boring. I usually cut my remarks in half and cut out points that are not essential to my objective. I then practice a few times more.

I share this method with my students, but I urge them to experiment and find the method of preparation that works best for them. Some people can get up and give a splendid talk spontaneously, but I can't do it. I must prepare.

Part of preparation is knowing your opening. The first impression is vital. A strong, confident opening is crucial. I can't believe the number of students whose first word in a presentation is "Uh," "Well," "You know," or "Okay." And, of course, you must know your close. Murphy's Law (anything that can go wrong, will go wrong) is always a threat, and so you must be prepared to bring your talk to a conclusion at any time. Being prepared and knowing your objective help you to conclude smoothly, even when you are cut short.

Aristotle

Since leadership is an influence process, leaders must know how to persuade. Most of their public speaking will contain an element of persuasion. Aristotle dealt with this issue in his *Rhetoric* over 2,000 years ago. I first became aware of Aristotle's insights from Mortimer Adler (*How to Speak How to Listen*), and I have been sharing his approach with my students for a number of years. The three basic elements of persuasion are the Greek words, *ethos*, *pathos*, and *logos*.

Ethos is primarily a person's character. Our word, ethics, comes from *ethos*, and it implies honesty, integrity, trustworthiness.

Pathos is feeling or passion. Through feeling and passion you connect with an audience's emotions.

Logos is the actual words or logic—the facts, the reasons.

Many people in the academic world concentrate solely on *logos*. They think they can persuade others by the sheer force of their logical argument. It does not work because they have not established ethos and pathos. They have little credibility because they have not made an emotional connection with the audience.

In persuasion, *ethos* comes first. You must establish your credibility, your character. The audience should know enough about you to believe that you have the right to be there—that you have the integrity to be trustworthy and the experience to be competent. You can accomplish this through a proper introduction and through stories about yourself.

Once you deal with *ethos* you must establish *pathos*. You do this by being genuinely interested in your subject and in your audience. You should have a passion for your subject. This passion will give you energy and enthusiasm and help your emotional appeal with the audience. You should think of pathos both in terms of your subject and your audience. You must care about both.

Only after you have established *ethos* and *pathos* can you move to *logos*. The audience will now be ready to hear your argument, persuasion, or sales pitch. Here you must stay focused on your objective and not muck it up with a lot of unnecessary verbiage, a point I must remember, too.

The Three Vs

I usually do the following exercise with my students.

A spoken message has three basic elements: the verbal, the vocal, and the visual. The verbal is made up of the actual words you use. The vocal includes the intonation and projection of your voice. The visual is what the audience sees—your body language and facial expressions.

I ask the students to think about a speaker they have heard who was sending a mixed message—whose words and tone and body language were not in sync. Which of the three (verbal, vocal, visual) did they rely on most to determine what the speaker was really saying? They usually choose visual and vocal.

They are right. When we get an inconsistent message, according to a study done by Albert Mehrabian of UCLA, we rely overwhelmingly on the visual and vocal elements to determine its believability. Here are the results of the study:

- Verbal   7%
- Vocal   38%
- Visual   55%

No wonder *ethos* and *pathos* are so important. And no wonder body language and facial expressions are so important. All the more reason to be as natural, as animated, as enthusiastic as you can in your presentations. As my colleague, Lyle Sussman, says, "Don't be a Mount Rushmore with lips!"

A sense of humor is usually helpful. Especially if it is directed at yourself. I don't recommend telling jokes. You can too easily offend someone in the audience. If you must tell a joke, tell it on yourself. Laugh at yourself. If you lighten up and don't take yourself too seriously, you will almost always be more warmly received by the audience. A genuine smile warms you up and warms the audience up, too.

Obviously, it depends on the circumstances, but I think an effective presentation comes from the heart. Of course, you must use your mind to organize it and deal with the *logos*.

But if you want to influence, to persuade, then the message must come from the heart. It's got to be *you*. The best compliment I can get after a talk is, "You sure spoke from the heart." Let's face it. You ultimately communicate who you are.

14.

Presentations

Speak what we feel, not what we ought to say.
—King Lear

In my first individual meetings with students, one of the things I cover is public speaking. I give them a card and ask them to rate themselves on a scale of 0 to 5 as to how they feel about making an oral presentation. The scale goes from "panic" (0) to "love doing it" (5). I have learned that students can fool me. Some of them can give a fine, polished presentation and I think they are in great shape. I later find out that they have gone through sheer torture to get there—hours of practice and worry.

I not only want them to do a good job in public speaking, but I also want them to be able to do it without so much distress. When I know the experience they have and how they feel about public speaking, I can work with them more effectively and deal with them where they are now.

We then talk about the oral presentation that they will

be making in the class. I ask if they have come up with a subject. A lot of them have. But a surprisingly large number say something like, "I've thought about it, but can't come up with anything. All I do is work and go to school. I don't do anything that anyone would be interested in."

I then have to probe. "What do you *really* like to do?"

"That's the trouble. I lead a dull life."

"What turns you on?"

"I'm not sure."

These people are afraid of revealing themselves. They are controlled by what they believe others will think of them. They have suppressed their own feelings to such an extent that they don't even know what their feelings are.

I then explain what I am trying to do. "The class is about leadership, and leadership is an influence process. A leader influences others. We are always influenced through emotions, not by facts and figures. We have to connect with our listeners on a emotional level. My experience is that most of us—especially in business—go around wearing suits of armor. We hide our emotions—who we are and how we feel—behind our corporate masks. We play games in communicating to protect ourselves. That's why there is so much miscommunication in the typical organization.

"I am trying to help you become more effective in your oral presentations. To do that you must put something of yourself into the presentation. You must open up and reveal yourself. That's how you become a more effective communicator. Working only on technique will help you become a slicker presenter, but it won't necessarily make you more effective in influencing your listeners. So I want you to drop the corporate mask.

"A leader also goes first—takes the lead. I want you to take the lead in talking about something you are interested in and really care about. If you open up and reveal something of yourself—who you really are—then it will influence me to open up more and reveal something of myself. It's scary because you become vulnerable. But you must do it if you are going to effectively influence someone else. If everyone in the class opens up more honestly, then we will be communicating on a deeper, more meaningful level. We will create an atmosphere of trust where we can genuinely start learning from each other."

"Does that help you?" I ask.

"Yes."

"What are you thinking about for a subject now?"

The students bring up a couple of possible subjects, but are often still undecided. I probe some more and can usually tell what they are most interested in through their body language. Their faces light up when they hit the right subject. I then urge them to pursue that subject. They don't have to, but the choice is theirs.

Some students automatically think in terms of what is interesting to the audience. "You have it backwards," I reply. "You're letting the audience influence—even control—you. You must start with what is interesting to you—what you have some passion about. Then through your sincerity and enthusiasm you will be interesting to your audience."

So what do they talk about? Everything! I love the presentations. Over the years I have heard some remarkable stories and have gotten new insights into human nature. People seem more effective—have greater impact—when they reveal something unexpected about themselves. Many men, for instance, have talked about what fatherhood has meant to them. A number of my students have recently become fathers, and they have shared how this experience has transformed them. Some have been moved to tears. They are initially embarrassed about this display of emotion, but they soon realize that their peers do not think less of them because they have revealed this aspect of their being. Just the opposite is the case —greater understanding, empathy, and respect for having the courage not only to be themselves but to make themselves vulnerable.

The most dramatic father was John. He started his talk, left the room, came back with his four-month old daughter, and held her in his arms through the rest of his talk. An effective visual! And I did not mind that he occasionally lost eye contact with the audience.

A number of the women talk about motherhood. Women seem to be more at ease talking about relationships, and I have been deeply moved by their stories. Some stories that stick in my mind, however, were unexpected—stories about adventures the women had had that showed an aspect of themselves that they normally did not reveal. At least two women have done presentations on sky diving. One went parasailing on her honeymoon. Several have gone white water rafting. One had become an expert in tae kwon do. The common theme was that these women seemed to need excitement, adventure, and risk in their lives. Their stories were revealing.

What ultimately makes a memorable presentation, for my purposes, is telling a dramatic story—or stories. The story reveals something the audience did not know about the speaker. It does not have to be a heavy subject; it can be funny and amusing. But it must be revealing. When these speakers finish, we feel closer to them. Since we now know more about who they are we have greater trust in them, and in our future relationships we will probably listen to them more carefully.

One of the finest examples of this self-revelation was my colleague Terry. He was the last speaker in his group in a self-development program I conducted with faculty members.

He told an incredible story of when he had been a social worker and the young man he was responsible for had brutally murdered two men who had befriended him. It was tragic and a devastating experience for Terry. None of us in that room had heard the story before. It was powerful and filled with emotion. Terry showed us something of himself that none of us had seen. Our attitude towards him was changed forever. He revealed a depth of character that we had not been aware of. His impact on us was profound, and to this day I think we listen to him with a respect and trust that we did not have before.

Some other speakers, stories, and subjects that come to mind are Martha on an employee that worked for her who was dying of AIDS; Bill on coaching a soccer team and dealing with the death of one of his players; Kevin on the near death of his three-year-old daughter; Bev on taking care of her mother in the last year of her life; Gayle on her mother's death and what it meant to her; Barb on losing her job; Cindy on having to lay off employees in her department in a corporate downsizing; Bill on pulling up stakes and traveling across the country as a hippie in a converted bus that looked like a portable shanty; Stephanie on her amazing spiritual journey to discover herself; and Richard and Robert (one graduate, one undergraduate) who in different classes in the same semester talked about their struggle with alcoholism.

I have found that I can help participants improve their communication skills more effectively by working on the "personal." When I started teaching, I would let students and executives talk on technical business subjects in their area of expertise. Often they would present a shortened version of a presentation that they had made in their businesses. These presentations permitted the speakers to hide behind their subjects. They could give a slick performance, but they made no emotional connection with the audience. They had little passion, and the audience got no insight into who the speaker really was. Until speakers were willing to reveal emotions and feelings, they were not going to be effective in influencing and persuading others.

The best example of this influence process took place in an Effective Executive program several years ago. Don was one of the first speakers, and he talked about the difficulty of being a divorced father permitted to see his children only once a week. His children were young—seven and nine —and he missed them dreadfully. He described how they would do things together and how special it was when they came over to his apartment to spend the night. He said that it might sound corny but what he really liked was having them get in bed with him and watch a certain TV show. He ended his talk by saying, "When you go home tonight, be sure to tuck your children in bed and tell them good night. Tell them how much you love them."

Well, there wasn't a dry eye in the place—except for Don. He seemed totally composed. Hell, I was crying—we all were. We were deeply touched. Don had done a masterful job, but in a completely natural way. He simply told his story, with great humor and poise and without a trace of self-pity.

Everyone who followed Don—both that night and the next week—changed their talk. They made their talks more "personal," shared something on a much deeper level than they had planned. One of them later said to me, "I could not give what I had planned to say after Don's talk. It would have sounded so shallow. I had to be more open and honest."

At the session the following week, it was heartwarming to see the number of people who said to Don, "I want you to know that when I went home last week I put my children to bed and gave them a special hug."

And in that next session one of the executives, the controller of a large company, in direct response to Don's presentation, talked about the pain he had suffered being the child of divorced parents and growing up having to live with visiting rights and how it had affected his relationship with his father. Later he told me that he had never talked about this subject to anyone, and, of course, had never made this kind of talk in his life. When he viewed the videotape, he was amazed and pleasantly surprised at how effectively he had communicated. All he had ever done before in a presentation was to give out the numbers. Now he realized he could do a lot more. He could become more than a technician. He had the potential to be a leader: he could influence others.

Because of what Don did and how he did it, he caused everyone who followed him to change their approach. The result was the best series of presentations of any of the groups I have worked with.

What makes Don stand out in my memory is not only the presentation itself, but the timing of it. Don went at the beginning; he was one of the first speakers. With sixteen presentations, I schedule eight the first week and eight the second. Usually when a speaker takes a big risk, such as Don, and gets into the personal and emotional, he or she holds off and tends to go near the end of the second week. The problem with that is that there is no one to follow. These people have a tremendous impact on the group, but since the others have already given their talks, the opportunity to influence them to change their approach has gone.

When I met with Don to review his tape, he was not aware of the tremendous impact he had made. In fact, when he watched the tape he was somewhat dubious about his performance, and he found numerous weaknesses in his presentation. Even after I praised the presentation and told him it was perhaps the best I had ever seen, he was still modest and unaware that he had done anything special.

This unawareness is a trait I have subsequently found in those people who have made outstanding presentations. They just talk about what they deeply care about—from the heart—not thinking about "performing." They usually re-live an experience through the stories they tell, and they connect totally with the audience. They don't think they have done anything special. In some cases they have even felt that they did a poor job and had blown it. It is hard for them to see how effective they were in the presentation from viewing the tape.

When you see yourself on the tape, it is such an intimate view of yourself that you cannot be objective. You need someone else—someone with experience—to give you an evaluation that you can believe is realistic.

What I am trying to do in these presentations is to get students and executives to think differently about oral presentations. Once they get more comfortable with revealing their feelings, they can communicate more effectively. Obviously, this approach must be tempered by the situation, but in most business presentations that I have listened to, a lighter touch, more illustrations and stories, and a more natural delivery are almost always welcomed by the audience. This does not mean that you don't have to be prepared. You must know what your point is and you must make it in the allotted time. But you must make it so that the audience will understand it and remember it.

Nothing pleases me more than when a student tells me that he made a presentation at work and his peers or his boss told him how good it was. When students learn from the experience of giving oral presentations in my class, and apply what they learn in their other public speaking requirements, they become more confident and more effective. When former students—who had dreaded public speaking—tell me with great pride of a successful presentation they have made at work, it is music to my ears. When they thank me for my help, it gives me that wonderful feeling that all teachers love. It's why we are teachers; we have helped a student learn how to be more effective.

15.

Videotaping

Oh wad some power the giftie gie us
To see oursels as others see us!
—Robert Burns

To see ourselves as the audience sees us is the most powerful learning tool available. If you want to improve your oral presentations, videotaping is essential. Everything else pales in comparison.

I don't understand why it took me so long to learn this fact. I even came from a television background. I didn't start taping my students' presentations until the fall of 1986, after I had been teaching for more than two years. One of my excuses for not taping was logistics. The equipment was not easy to come by or to use, tapes were expensive, and it was a lot of trouble getting things set up through the university audio-visual facilities.

I finally bit the bullet and operated the camera myself. As in so many cases when there have been logistical problems, the students came up with the best ways for handling them. I had a question about the videotape. A student suggested that each person bring his or her own cassette. That solved that problem.

Then students started asking for more than one taping. That put a demand on the limited equipment we had at the School. I finally bought my own camcorder, which gives me complete flexibility. I now tape each student five times a semester. This was not my idea; it was the students' request. The students are responsible for their own cassette. They have a record of all their presentations and can review it to see their progress and where they still need to improve.

For the first presentation (approximately five minutes) I ask the students to close by asking, "Are there any questions?" Then for about two minutes or so, they take questions from the audience (the other students). I let the tape keep running so that the students can see both their prepared presentation and their spontaneous responses to questions. If one segment is significantly better than the other, we must figure out how to get the weaker performance up to the higher level.

Conferences

After I tape the first oral presentation, I keep the tape. I want the student to look at it with me first. If you have never seen yourself on tape before, you can become hypercritical and can self-destruct. I want to make sure that the first time you see the tape, you will not become too critical of yourself and that you look for positives on which to build. In all tapings after the first one, students keep their tapes and review them on their own.

Before I started reviewing tapes with students, I thought I should learn something about how to give feedback, what to look for, and what to emphasize to get the most improvement. I taped myself and had my colleague, Lyle Sussman, review the tape with me, treating me just like a client he was consulting with. Seeing myself on tape and then reviewing it with a professional expert was a revealing experience. I subsequently used many of Lyle's techniques and have added my own as I have worked with students, executives, and colleagues.

Most students are nervous when they come into my office to view the tape. In many cases they have not seen themselves before, and they are expecting the worst. I try to look at the tape before the student gets there, but often I do not have time and am seeing the tape for the first time, right along with the student.

I explain, "We will view the entire tape including the question and answer part. I will ask you to look at the tape in a couple of different ways. When it is finished, I will ask you several questions. Then I will give you feedback and you can ask me any questions. Okay?"

"Okay."

"When you think about the presentation you gave, what was your objective, what did you want to leave the group with?"

If the answer is brief and to the point, the presentation is usually focused and cohesive. If the answer is vague, the presentation itself is usually not clear, but uneven and disjointed.

I then play the tape. After a couple of minutes I ask the student, "Now look away. Don't look at the picture. Just listen. Note the voice and tone and think about what you are hearing."

We do that for about thirty seconds. "All right. Now look at the screen." I turn off the volume. "Let's look at your body language and facial expressions without the sound." We do that for about thirty seconds.

When the tape ends I ask a series of questions.

• "Looking at the tape from as disinterested a view as

possible—from the audience's point of view—what would you say is the greatest strength of that presentation?"

Some students can give me an immediate answer, others have great difficulty. They want me to answer it. I keep asking. Reluctantly, they come forth with an answer, hoping that it will meet with my approval.

Ironically, I have found that academics have the hardest time with this question. I have done several programs with professors and administrators and when I ask them, they reply, "I don't see any strength. I see lots of weaknesses."

I then say, "I didn't ask you that. What is the strength of that presentation?"

They smile and often realize that their academic training has caused them to focus solely on the negative. I'm sure this attitude gets carried over into teaching, which is unfortunate because it is not the best way to help a student become more confident and competent in speaking.

• "What one thing would you like to do that would bring about the biggest improvement in the presentation?"

I am trying to get them to concentrate on only one thing. Most of us can do only one thing at a time. The trick is to figure out what will make the biggest difference or improvement, and then work on that. Trying to work on several things at once seldom brings about meaningful improvement.

• "Any observations or comments about the sound—what you heard when you focused on the voice?"

• "How about your body language and facial expression? Either when we turned the sound off or at other times."

• "When you looked at the presentation part, and then the question and answer part, did you think you did better in one than the other?"

After students answer this last question, I like to give them my response to the presentation. I am always positive. I can always find something good—a strength—in the presentation. If the presentation is good, I let the student know how good I think it is. That's always fun. The student's face lights up, there's a smile, and a warm "Thank you." Even if the presentation is not particularly good, I find something in which the student can be pleased and feel good about. Students who are weak in speaking must first of all gain some self-confidence. They must leave my office realizing that they are not as bad as they thought they were, and they can see how they can improve.

I then review their responses to my questions. I usually agree with what they consider to be the greatest strength. The one thing that would bring about the greatest improvement is more difficult to agree on, but after discussion we usually have a clear understanding of what that is and what the student will concentrate on in the future.

Similar points often come up when we discuss the voice. A lot of people, including me, don't like the sound of their voice when they hear it on tape. Most of my students are from Kentucky, and they are shocked at their accents when they first hear themselves. I don't worry about the accent. I think it is better to speak in your natural way, rather than to try to change your accent. This advice has helped my international students. "Stop worrying about your accent and just concentrate on your message, using natural animation in your body and facial expressions," I tell them.

The biggest complaint about the voice is that it is too monotone. "The best way to get more animation in your voice is to get more animation in your body and face. It's impossible to get animation in your voice when your facial muscles are tight. Relax and smile."

Other points we agree on regarding the voice are the need for more pauses, for fewer guttural utterances during pauses ("uh," "you know"), and in some cases talking too fast.

The response to my question on body language is mixed. Some students have been told not to use their hands so much. I ask them if the hand gestures bothered them when they viewed the tape. They almost always answer, "No."

"Then don't even think about your hands during a presentation. Let your hands do what they would naturally do in conversation. The worst thing is to become self-conscious and jam your hands in your pockets the whole time or clasp them behind your back."

Some students are worried that they move around too much. I don't worry about that. Movement adds energy—you just don't want to rock back and forth in one place.

Students can readily see how well they make eye contact. What often happens is that they look down—and talk down—to notes more than they should. On tape you can quickly see how ineffective that is.

Overwhelmingly, most students feel that they are too stiff and tight in their body language and facial expressions. I don't have to tell them anything. They know they must loosen up.

In this kind of presentation, most students feel they do a better job in the question-and-answer segment than in the prepared presentation. I agree with them and think there are two basic reasons.

All of us, no matter how professional we are, go "Whew!" when we finish a presentation. We relax and loosen up. The audience senses it and also becomes more comfortable. We are all more at ease, creating greater rapport.

The second reason is that when a person asks us a question, we listen and focus on that person. We make direct eye contact and answer him or her directly, momentarily forgetting we are talking to a group. We go into our one-on-one conversational mode. This is the style we use the most and are most comfortable with. So we become more natural—and more effective.

A man I worked with in the Effective Executive program was in a high executive position in one of Louisville's largest corporations. He had a phobia about public speaking.

He made his presentation to the class and was obviously nervous. When we reviewed the tape he said that he could never speak comfortably before a group. I told him he already had. I then replayed the question-and-answer segment. He answered the questions beautifully, fully in command and completely at ease. He had forgotten he was addressing a group and instead was just talking one-on-one to individuals.

"When you get up there next time, remember you are just talking one-on-one with individuals—just like you do in everyday conversations. You have shown that you can do that with great skill."

I've seldom seen such relief in a person's face. He said this was the most helpful advice he had received, and he thanked me profusely.

It took me a long time to recognize the fundamental difference between the written word and the spoken word. I used to think that a good speech required the same elements as a good article. In other words, a good memo would make a good oral presentation. Wrong! They are entirely different.

Writing falls apart without a clear structure. It must be organized and carefully edited. It proceeds in a linear fashion, word by word, sentence by sentence, with smooth transitions from paragraph to paragraph.

Speaking does not work that way. Spontaneity and emotion have greater impact than the precise organization of the content. That's why stories are so important. Your stories build the connection between your content and your audience.

The written document is a product that you produce. It exists apart from you. The readers can read it over and over and can read it at their own pace. A spoken presentation takes place in real time. It is not a product you produce; it is you. You are the message.

In working with students, I began to realize that I had to treat their written work differently from their oral work. I could criticize the writing and put grades on it because I was evaluating and grading the product, not the person. Students were relatively open to suggestions about improving a product.

This approach did not work for oral presentations. Students always felt that they were being judged, not their work. A poor grade demoralized a weak performer and made that performer even less confident. I realized that I had to help bolster my students' self-confidence if they were going to improve. I don't know which comes first, confidence or competence. I do know you need to have both. I try to improve both, but have found it hard to improve the competence without improving the confidence right along with it.

So that is why I don't grade the oral presentations. And that is why I do everything I can to have a student feel good about himself or herself after seeing that first presentation. We can all improve, but we have to believe we can before we will do the work necessary to improve.

Incidentally, several of my colleagues were skeptical of my not grading the oral presentations. "Students won't work hard if they are not graded. They will just do the minimum to get by," they claimed.

I have found this opinion totally erroneous. If anything, I have found the students work harder and smarter—and are more willing to receive criticism and try something new—when they are not being graded. Students, like most people, want to do good work. And they have their pride; nobody wants to look bad in front of others.

For those students who have been worried about their nervousness, I ask, "Now that you have seen the tape, did you appear as nervous on the tape as you felt when you were making the presentation?" The answer is always "No." This is one of the great advantages of videotape. You see yourself as the audience sees you. The audience isn't looking for your nervousness. They are not aware of it. The audience only gets what you give them.

It's great to be able to tell a student, "Whenever you give an oral presentation—for the rest of your life—you will never appear as nervous to the audience as you feel to yourself." The fear that an audience focuses on our nervousness is excess baggage that many of us carry around, and now we can get rid of it—forever.

16.

Reading

*Reading maketh a full **man**;*
conference a ready man;
and writing an exact man.
　　　　—Francis Bacon

Reading maketh a full person;
conference a ready person;
writing an exact person;
and listening a caring person.
　　—Ballard's politically correct version

In one of the early classes we have a discussion about reading. Improving reading skills is one of the objectives of the class. Although there are a number of exceptions, I have found that many of my students don't like to read. I would go further: they don't know how to read. At least, how to read to get the maximum benefit for themselves.

　　This aversion to reading is understandable. After all, most of my students' exposure to serious reading is the text book. If this were my principal exposure to reading, I wouldn't like it either. Students have been forced to read text books, and, worse, forced to memorize data and passages from them that they must recall on a subsequent test. The object then becomes to read and memorize for the test. After the test, the subject matter is largely forgotten. Under such circumstances, no real learning takes place.

I want to hook my students on reading, and I want them to learn how to read selfishly—that is, for their own self-interest. Paul Valéry's observation is so true: "One only reads well that which one reads with some quite personal purpose." The students need to engage the author and the book. They need to think about what the author is saying and how it might affect themselves, or how it might be useful in their careers or daily lives.

They must drop the mindset of reading for the test, or reading for the professor. They must learn to think about what they are reading and open up their imagination and curiosity and become receptive to new ideas and new insights. Such an approach to reading is a broadening experience, and it can lead to greater understanding. It's also fun.

I recently came across a useful technique to help us become more engaged with the author. In *The Western Canon*, Harold Bloom refers to "a crucial question we should ask of any writer in whom we read deeply: What would the author think of us?" I find this approach intriguing. As I reread *The Effective Executive*, for instance, I wonder what Peter Drucker would think of me—my ability to understand what he is saying, to think about what it means, and to put his suggestions into practice.

The possibilities are even more wide-open when I apply this question to Machiavelli or to Shakespeare. How would they describe what we are doing in class? The question stimulates some imaginative thinking, allowing us to get more value from our reading.

I am an avid reader. I read all the time. Sometimes

reading for me is more than a divertissement; it's an escape. I don't want my students to go that far. But surely they can strike a balance.

One of the problems I see is television. I grew up before television was so prevalent. In my youth when I was alone my primary entertainment was reading. Reading requires you to engage with the printed word. You must create ways of looking and seeing with your own imagination. To read effectively, your mind must be active. Television does not require an active mind and imagination. You can sit, passively, and let the words and pictures on the tube do it all for you. Unfortunately, students bring this passivity to a book and conclude that it's too hard or they don't get it. They don't know how to get it because they approach it the same way they approach watching a television program.

For a number of years I made my living in television. The passive nature of television viewing bothered me then, and it bothers me now. There are many good things about television. But the fact remains, watching television and reading are entirely different activities. Especially in those formative years, the former works against the latter.

The class is hardly a course in the Great Books or classics, although I would love to teach a course on leadership using literary classics through the ages. Instead, we read ten books, including a play, and a number of articles. Two of the books would be considered classics, *The Prince* and either *Antigone* or a Shakespeare tragedy. The rest are books that I think are helpful to the students in improving their skills and understanding as they develop their leadership potential.

I tell the students they don't need to read every word of every book. That is not an effective use of their time. They should read with the idea of understanding what the author is saying, and, when it is relevant to them, they should think deeply about it and explore how they can put this new knowledge or understanding to use in their lives. I want them to consider the author as another guest we have invited to the class. What can I learn from this person?

The subsequent class discussions make the reading more worthwhile. Having to express your opinion makes you think more carefully about what you have read and about your attitude toward it. Hearing other views opens all kinds of new vistas and gives you insights you would never have otherwise had. I am constantly astounded at the different views and approaches my students have toward a book or article. These views cause me to think again or look at the issue from a new point of view. In these situations, I truly learn from my students.

At a minimum, the student must read enough of the book—must think about it enough—to write a thoughtful memo on it. Nearly all the future written assignments are memos based on the assigned reading. Generally, students write better memos when they read the book early, think about it for a day or so, and then decide what they want to write. Seldom is a memo effective or well-expressed without some hard thinking before the words get on paper.

At the end of every semester, I give the students a reading list, "Ballard's Bibliophily" (see Appendix III). This is an eclectic list of some twenty books that I continually update. These are not necessarily books on leadership, but many are. They are simply books I like and have found stimulating. Former students often ask about my reading list, and they suggest books for me to read, too.

In my final assessment with the students, there are always a few who tell me that I have reawakened them to the joys and benefits of reading. That is music to my ears, because when they know how to read good books—and they continue to read them—they will continue to learn and grow.

Learning to read selfishly, imaginatively, thoughtfully is one way to learn how to learn.

17.

Listening

Lord, grant that I may seek not so much
to be understood as to understand.
—Prayer of Saint Francis

For several years when I was with Orion Broadcasting I interviewed everyone who reported to the general manager in each of our stations. This worked out to more than fifty interviews each year. I quickly learned that if the interview was to be beneficial, I had to listen with great care and skill.

I had no training in how to interview or how to listen, but I had a strong desire to learn what was going on in our stations from the employee's point of view. The employee's perception was the reality I wanted to understand. I found that I had to listen with my eyes. The employee's body language often told me more than the actual words.

I asked employees about their relationship with their boss and what trait or behavior they would most like to see their boss change. Often the answer was, "To listen better."

You don't have to be a rocket scientist to figure out

that listening is the key to effective communication. Yet we don't teach people how to listen, and there is relatively little in the way of literature on listening or how to teach listening. I knew from the outset that I wanted to do a segment on listening in my class, but the problem was what material to use.

Fortunately, I found two brochures from the Sperry Corporation called "How important it is to Listen" and "Your Personal Listening Profile." We used these in my first classes, and they were helpful. The Listening Profile had a quiz in it where you rate yourself as a listener and then have others rate you, such as people you work with, your best friend, your spouse. The scale was from 0-100 (100 = highest), from terrible to average to superior.

I had remarried at the end of my first year of teaching, and I remember taking the quiz home to my new wife, Muff. I knew that I would have gotten an extremely low rating from my former spouse, but this was different. I had learned so much about listening, and I was certain that I had become a much better listener. Much to my shock Muff rated me a 20. The honeymoon was over. I told myself, if you don't want to hear the answer, then don't ask the question. Actually, this was helpful, but painful, feedback. Muff has taught me a lot about listening, and she is good at pointing out when I don't listen well—especially to her and to my children. It is one thing to know how to listen; it is quite another thing to do it. Why is it that I seem to do the worst job of listening to those I love the most?

In our class discussion on listening, I had the students talk about their ratings on the quizzes. I shared my results with them, and they always got a laugh out of my spouse's rating of me. My willingness to share this woeful assessment with them helped to set a healthy climate in the class. My honesty and openness made it easier for others to be more honest and open. And my low rating showed that I wasn't any better than the students were, that I didn't know any more than they did about listening. I was certainly no expert. This meant that we were all in the same boat and could learn together.

I got a real surprise in my second graduate class. I did the session on listening using the Sperry brochures. The next morning I got a call from one of the older students, Mike. "Ballard, I sandbagged you last night."

"What do you mean?"

"I know a fair amount about listening. I've had quite a bit of training, and, as a matter of fact, I have conducted workshops in listening."

"You don't say!"

"As Director of the Presbyterian Children's Home, I have run a number of workshops in listening skills for parents. We cover much the same material the brochures do. I'd be willing to conduct a workshop on listening for the class—maybe an hour or so. Would you be interested?"

"You bet I would. Could you do it in class next week?"

"Yes, I'll be glad to, and I'll bring some materials to hand out."

So, at the next class session, I told the class about Mike's offer, and then I turned the class over to him. He ran the workshop, and I participated as a student. It was quite a learning experience for me. Perhaps the greatest lesson I learned was in our role playing. I found that it is extremely hard to listen to someone without interrupting or judging.

Another lesson I learned is to always ask in each class —before we start discussing listening—if there is anyone in the class who has had training in listening. If so, I want them to teach us what they know. I tell them the story of my experience with Mike.

In the fall of 1986 I was browsing in a bookstore and came across a small paperback, *I Hear You*, by Eastwood Atwater. I had been on the lookout for a book on listening, and so I bought it. I read it and liked it and told my students about it when we discussed listening in class. One of them said to me, "That sounds like a good book. Why don't you have it as one of your assigned books for the class?" That made sense and I have been using it ever since. (Unfortunately, at this writing the book is out of print, and I am getting copyright permission to have copies made for my students.)

Most of us have not had any instruction in how to listen. When we first went to school we spent a lot of time learning how to read and write, and we got some instruction in how to speak correctly. But nothing on how to listen. The only instruction I ever got was, "Shut up and pay attention!" Now that may not have been bad advice, but it did not teach me how to listen.

There is a paradox when it comes to formal schooling and listening. Most of our waking time is spent communicating—listening, speaking, reading, and writing. The Sperry Listening Profile presents a chart showing that listening is the communication skill we learn first and use the most, but are taught the least.

	Listening	**Speaking**	**Reading**	**Writing**
Learned	1st	2nd	3rd	4th
Used	Most	Next Most	Next Least	Least
	(45%)	(30%)	(16%)	(9%)
Taught	Least	Next Least	Next Most	Most

Why is this? I think one reason is that academia does not want to teach anything that cannot be tested. It is difficult, if not impossible, to test listening effectiveness. You can test memory, but not empathic understanding. And if you can't test it, you can't teach it—or so the thinking goes.

To understand more about listening, you need to consider the other side of the equation. Why do people talk to each other? Most analyses conclude that there are four purposes: social, informative, persuasive, and emotional or expressive. Sometimes speakers are not sure of their purpose in talking, or they have several purposes, which means that as a listener you have a harder job ferreting out the meaning, and you must pay attention to all the nonverbal clues.

You must adapt your listening to the speaker's purpose. You must understand what the speaker is trying to do and adjust your listening appropriately. Obviously, we listen differently in a social, small-talk conversation than when our boss is giving us instructions or explaining a new policy.

The area I concentrate on in my class is in the emotional or expressive category. This is the area where we can make the greatest difference in our relationships, both in our work and in our personal lives.

I give the students a two-page handout on listening that I put together in 1991. I draw on the work of Carl Rogers and Stephen Covey, and what I particularly stress is listening with empathy or empathic listening. Listening at its deepest level means trying to see things the way the speaker sees them. At this level listening involves empathy, which is *experiencing with* the speaker. Empathy also means *understanding with* another person.

To be able to listen and understand from the other person's point of view is extremely difficult. It is not a technique you can learn. It comes from your attitude and it starts with your attitude toward yourself. You must know who you are, what you believe in, your own feelings. You must be accepting of yourself and the speaker. You must have self-confidence and courage. Yes, courage, because when we listen with empathy, with understanding with the other person, we take a huge risk. We risk being influenced and changed. You must have a strong sense of character—who you are—and confidence in order to take that risk.

Listening with empathy implies a suspension of evaluation and judgment. It implies an acceptance of and respect for another person without having to agree with that person's views.

The problem is that most of us don't listen with the intent to understand. We listen with the intent to reply—reading our autobiography into other people's lives. We *evaluate* (either agree or disagree); we *probe* (ask questions from our own frame of reference); we *advise* (give counsel based on our own experience); and we *interpret* (figure people out based on our own motives and behavior).

Most of us usually listen at one of four levels:

1. Ignoring.
2. Pretending ("Yeah," "Uh huh," "Right").
3. Selective listening (hearing only certain parts of the conversation).
4. Attentive listening (focusing on the words).

We rarely get to the fifth level—the highest form of listening—empathic listening (understanding how the other person feels).

To help the students focus on this aspect of their listening, I give them this assignment for their memo: "Study the chapters on empathic listening in *I Hear You*. Then listen to someone with the intent to really understand that person— what he or she is saying and feeling. Don't judge; don't interrupt. Just listen. Write a memo describing the experience from your point of view. What did you learn about yourself and about listening? What was the effect on the speaker?"

I have been doing this assignment for six years, and it has proven to be of real benefit to most students in helping them become more aware of their listening habits. Students discuss in class what they discovered in doing this exercise, and the results are sometimes amusing, sometimes touching, and sometimes transforming.

Invariably several students share the experience of listening to their spouses. Usually the spouse realizes something has changed, and usually the spouse likes the change—likes the way he or she is being listened to. Then there is the dilemma. Do you tell your spouse that this is part of an exercise you are doing for class, or do you just remain silent and learn from the experience and try to change your listening behavior in the future? I have learned not to give advice in these situations.

Some students tell about listening to a parent or elderly relative. They confess that this was the first time they had ever really listened to that person, and they were amazed at what happened. They understood and appreciated that person in a way they never had before. They realize that their empathic listening had affected both the speaker and themselves—sometimes on a deeply emotional level.

The vast majority of students say that the exercise has made them aware of their normal listening habits. They usually want to judge, interrupt, inject their own opinions, think about what they want to say, or finish the other person's sentences. Above all they learn that empathic listening is hard work. It takes tremendous concentration. Listening is the most difficult of the communication skills because we must concentrate on someone else and stay at that person's pace. Our mind wants to race ahead and think about a lot of other things.

The exercise is also difficult because it feels awkward. You are asked to do something you don't normally do and asked at the same time to observe and analyze the speaker's behavior and your own behavior. But doing the exercise can make a tremendous difference in your learning about yourself. Previously I had the students write a memo describing some aspect of listening that is analyzed in the book. No matter what they wrote it did not make much difference in their subsequent listening behavior. This new exercise requires them to do something. They get involved and this involvement helps them learn. It helps them learn more about themselves and shows them what they must learn to do if they are to become more effective listeners.

Here are some verbatim excerpts from their memos:

• I believe I made strides toward improving my listening skills during this exercise. I asked my husband about this after the conversation ended. He agreed that I had been attentive, that I had interrupted less, and that I did not attempt to finish his sentences quite as often. However, because I had told him I needed to have this conversation for a school project, I am not sure his feelings about the conversations were as positive as mine.

• I became aware of how hard I had to work at not being judgmental. It is apparent that I need an attitude adjustment as much as I thought the speaker did.

• I was shocked to realize how much I have to learn and practice on the "art" of listening. I was constantly tempted to interrupt and prompt her during the conversation. I also realized that I have the tendency to judge what is being said to me. I really worked at stepping into her shoes and sending non-verbal clues that I was listening. Just this brief experiment has really opened my eyes.

• From the above experience and having read *I Hear You*, I realize I have a few faults in listening that I plan on improving. I had to hold myself back from injecting my point of view. I usually try to relate my experiences with the speaker's, when I should be considerate and "hear" the person out. I judge people and situations prematurely. I need to take the time to hear the whole story. This will be challenging, because I know I'm impatient and jump to conclusions.

• Normally, I would have interrupted the speaker when I thought I understood the problem. But by remaining quiet I learned that she already had an answer and simply wanted my approval. This gave her empowerment and respect. I went from a position of power to one of neutrality. Instead of dictating an answer, I was able to objectively listen to her problem, which is really what she wanted.

• It was an enlightening experience to actively listen to my mother speak. I found myself soaking in each word and for the first time allowing those words to linger in my mind as I tried empathetically to understand how she felt. The change in my listening habits must have been evident to her. I noticed that she spoke more softly, slowly, and did not repeat herself as she had in past conversations. I noticed how vulnerable we both were as we allowed prior guards to fall. For the first time, I actually felt my mother's pain and frustration. I did little talking, yet it was the best conversation I can ever remember having with her.

• My daughter and I both felt better. She felt better because I gave her my full attention. I felt better because I really understood what she was trying to tell me. It reminded me of what someone told me a long time ago. When a child comes to an adult with a problem, we have a tendency to downgrade the problem by comparing it to what we perceive as real problems. If we try to look at the problem through the child's eyes and understand their feelings, we quickly find their problem is as serious to them as our adult problems are to us.

• This was a difficult exercise for me. I believe that I can be more effective in all aspects of communication if I improve my listening skills. But it cannot be forced. If I'm thinking about how to listen and whether I'm doing a good job, I won't really be listening. I hope to change my listening habits by applying the techniques described in Atwater's book, and I plan to review this exercise at the end of the semester to see if I've been successful.

• The conversation went into more depth than usual and I

could tell she appreciated my interest. There were several major distractions, however. The biggest was due to the assignment itself. Even though I was trying to concentrate on everything she said, I caught myself critiquing my listening "performance."... Despite the less-than-perfect ending, I could tell she appreciated my improved efforts at listening. Reading through Atwater's book opened my eyes to just how easily you can begin to improve your listening skills. Perfecting these skills, however, will take many months of practice.

Ultimately, I think we communicate to get a response from someone else. To the degree that we don't know what response we want, our communication will be poor. We won't connect. To be a good communicator, we must know the response we want, and then we must be perceptive enough to notice whether or not we are getting it. If we are not, we must be flexible enough to change and express ourselves in a different way—so that we connect. The amazing thing about most of us is that when we find something that does not work, we keep doing it, only trying harder.

What has this to do with listening? Everything. Listening is fundamentally a response. Becoming a good listener means learning how to respond to another person. It's the basis of any relationship, and relationships are what leadership is built upon. As a speaker, you must be able to "listen" to your audience; you must respond to your audience. You must be perceptive and sensitive to their response or lack of response and change your behavior accordingly. A good listener develops this sensitivity—and ironically becomes a more effective speaker. Effective speaking and listening are an integral part of each other. As Stephen Covey says, the key to effective interpersonal communication is "Seek first to understand, then to be understood."

18.

Peter Drucker

Up to this point the focus of the course has been on communications. It makes sense to cover communications at the beginning so that students can work on these skills throughout the semester. As obvious as this is, it took the students to point it out to me. I used to spread the assignments in communications somewhat randomly, and some students said that it would be better to concentrate on communications up front.

We next read Peter Drucker's *The Effective Executive*. There is no mysterious reason why it comes here; it just felt right to me to read it at this point. It requires a great deal of concentration by the reader, and I want the students to engage it relatively early in the semester when they still have a high level of energy. Besides, they can immediately start working on putting his suggestions into practice—both at school and at work. I read *The Effective Executive* when it was first published in 1967. I liked it so much that I wrote up a summary and analysis of it, which I distributed to all my managers.

In my first class, I had a team of three students read the book and then present the highlights to the rest of the class. One of the students suggested I make it required reading for the class. It was easy to accept this suggestion, and *The Effective Executive* has been a mainstay in all my classes ever since. It's even the name I chose for the executive program Bob Taylor and I conduct.

Peter Drucker is remarkable. He is in his late 80s and keeps going and going, and writing and writing. He has had more than thirty articles published in the *Harvard Business Review*. No one else even comes close. And no one understands effectiveness better than he does. He sees things more clearly than the rest of us. Although *The Effective Executive* is a bit dated now, the advice is still valid and to the point. It's just 174 pages, loaded with examples, insights, and predictions of many things that have come to pass.

Drucker's style is difficult for some students and executives. English is not his first language. He had a classical European education and uses some unfamiliar terms. Some of his phrasing is awkward, and he often writes in the passive voice. This is definitely not the easy read of *How to Get Your Point Across*. But it is worth the effort.

The book was written three decades ago. Everything in business writing at that time was written using only the masculine gender. Writers always referred to a manager or leader as "he." Drucker was no exception. The book seems sexist to the contemporary reader. I point this out to my students and they seem to understand the situation. Drucker, in his current writing uses "he or she," but *The Effective Executive* has not been revised even in its newer editions.

Incidentally, I have found that 1972 was the turning-point year. Business writing published before 1972 nearly always refers just to the masculine gender. After 1972, writers became more careful to indicate a manager or leader could be either male or female. Since I have the students read material published before 1972, I have to be careful to point this out. An obvious case is *The Prince.* I find that I need to be sensitive to this issue, and the best way is to discuss it openly—before the students read it.

The written assignment is a one-page executive summary of *The Effective Executive.* Reducing the book to one page is a challenge. Students have already had practice doing an executive summary (*How To Get Your Point Across*), and so they know what I am looking for. I ask them to write the summary in their own words, in the active voice, and to use second person personal pronouns or imperatives where possible. This allows the students to use "you" instead of "the effective executive," "he," or "one" throughout the memo. The memo is written to me, and I want them to tell me what Drucker says I should do to be effective. Writing in the second person is more direct, less formal, and easier to read.

In the book Drucker defines effectiveness as getting the right things done, and executives as knowledge workers who make decisions that affect the performance and results of the organization. He says that effectiveness is a habit that consists of five practices, and these practices can and must be learned. They are:

1. <u>Manage your time.</u> Record your time and analyze how you spend it. Manage it by eliminating things that do not need to be done at all, by delegating those things others could do just as well, and by pruning the time-wasters—especially the time of others that you waste. Then consolidate the discretionary time you have into large chunks so that you can concentrate your time on what is important.
2. <u>Focus on contribution.</u> Ask "What can I contribute that will make the greatest impact on my organization?"Always focus on results, not on your efforts. Focusing on your contribution provides the four basic elements of effective

human relations: communications, teamwork, self-development, and development of others.

3. Build on strengths.   Make staffing decisions and promotions to maximize people's strengths, not to minimize their weaknesses.   Build on your own strengths and those of the people you work with. Focus on opportunities rather than problems. Make sure you know the results you want and then demand performance. Get rid of non-performers.

4. Concentrate on priorities. Work on the few major areas where you can produce outstanding results. Do first things first—one at a time—and second things not at all. Have the courage to go after opportunities.

5. Make effective decisions. Decision-making is a systematic process, and you should make few, but fundamental, decisions. An effective decision is a judgment based on dissenting opinions and requires you to follow through with appropriate action.

In writing a summary of the book in their own words, students become more familiar with the five practices. In class I do a further exercise. I have them form groups, share their memos and ideas with each other, and then select one spokesperson to give a one-minute consensus summary of the book to the rest of the class. The students also give each other feedback on these presentations.

I recently got an audio tape of an interview with Drucker on *The Effective Executive*. The interview was done 25 years after the book was published and gives Drucker's current views. Drucker is still enthusiastic about the book, and the tape helps bring the book to life. His views have not changed that much, but he does say that he is now more modest about how much time an executive can get control of in the typical organization.

We always have a stimulating discussion of the points in the book. Drucker's insights are right on the mark, whether they be on meetings, performance appraisals, or the need for diversity in the workplace. His observations are all the more impressive in that they have held up over time. Every student in my classes wants to become more effective. Drucker shows them how—and what they must start doing now. There is no reason why they can't start now.

My observation—of both students and executives—is that most of us don't think about effectiveness and how we can be more effective. We just stay busy, trying harder, and our schedule fills up with more to do than we have time to do it. Most of us think about our efforts—how hard we are working and how many hours we are putting in. We don't think about results. Yet results are what we get paid for. Results are all that matter to other people—especially customers. How many of us ask, "What can I contribute that will really make a difference?" Not many, I'm afraid. It's time to look into the mirror, and Drucker provides us the mirror.

The implications for me are obvious. If we want to become a more effective executive we must have greater awareness of our own strengths and abilities (self-knowledge) and have the courage and confidence to build on those strengths and the strengths of those we work with. We must think about the contribution we can make to our organization (results, not efforts). We must know our priorities and concentrate on them. We must stop doing those things that are no longer productive (don't get the desired results). We must welcome differing opinions (diversity) because only through disagreement can we make effective decisions. Above all, we must practice, practice, practice.

19.

Articles Exercise

In my early classes, I would randomly call on students to get up and present their memos to the class. Students had to be prepared to speak in every class. Some students dreaded this possibility. Invariably, one would say, "I was really prepared last week, but you didn't call on me." I didn't have much sympathy in these cases. Their job was to be prepared each week.

However, I began to see that my methods were inhibiting the students' learning. Some students sat in absolute fear of being called on. If they were called on, they would give their talk, then sit down in utter relief and not participate for the rest of the class. They had been totally preoccupied with their talk and felt that they had participated enough. This kind of behavior did not make for vigorous, free-flowing discussions.

What was the solution? Some students were requesting more videotaped presentations, and some were requesting more class discussion. Were these requests incompatible? As in so many cases, the students gave me the answers. We decided to do a couple of things differently.

First, (this would take place in classes later in the semester) I would assign certain students to make oral presentations (two and a half minutes) on their memos. They would know when they were to make these presentations and would bring their video cassettes. I have now modified this exercise further: they can present what is in their memos or they can talk about something else, as long as it is pertinent to the book we are discussing and stays within the two-and-a-half minute time limit. Previously, I had not taped these presentations, so they now get an additional taping.

Second, I created a group exercise that we do in the sixth class session. It sounds complicated, but it works. The students read four articles from the *Harvard Business Review*:

"What Leaders Really Do" by John P. Kotter;

"Ways Women Lead" by Judy B. Rosener;

"Moral Mazes: Bureaucracy and Managerial Work" by Robert Jackall; and

"Management Time: Who's Got the Monkey?" by William Oncken, Jr. and Donald L. Wass.

For their memos, students write one paragraph on each article, stating the main point of the article.

For the class exercise, I assign four students to each article. They get together as a group for just twenty minutes, discuss the article, and decide on the presentations they will make to the class. Each group makes presentations on its assigned article—each individual making a two-minute talk on some aspect of the article. I insist that one person present the article from the author's point of view; another present a contrary view (how would you argue against the author?); and the other two can be illustrations of the article based upon their personal experience. Each group must decide who is going to cover which aspect.

Each group makes its presentations to the class. Individuals have their own cassettes and I tape each presentation (a logistic feat that I awkwardly manage to pull off). After its four presentations, the group serves as a panel and leads the general discussion of the article. The whole process, presentations and discussion, always works better than I think it will. The students come through. It has been a win/win exercise for several reasons.

Students are focused on the articles. They have had to identify the main point, which means they have had to think about the article and what the author is saying. So often in academic assignments, students are asked to chase footnotes and analyze increasingly insignificant information in increasingly minute detail. The sound and fury, signifying nothing. They often miss the main point, because they are too busy analyzing trivial details. Here they are focused on the main point and have formed an opinion, and so they are prepared to have a more thoughtful discussion.

The students also get some experience working in a group. This is not technically a "team" effort, but they must work together and negotiate who is going to do what, compromise, and help each other out. They have little time to prepare their presentations, which is often the case in the business world. Just do it.

They get another chance to see themselves on videotape, which the majority has asked for. And they have a meaningful discussion of the main issues raised in the articles—without my control. Each group serves as the panel of experts and leads the discussion. The discussion is lively, and I stay in the background (maybe that's why it is lively!). I step in only to clarify an issue and to close off debate, so that we can move to the next group. The students take charge of their own learning, and in so doing they make the exercise meaningful to themselves and to each other.

20.

Discussion Leaders

About five or six years ago, I started the discussion leader project. This was a class in leadership, and I felt that students needed more practice in leading. It wasn't enough just to read about leadership and then discuss it. Students could learn more by doing.

I find it interesting in retrospect that the students in my first classes told me I tried to control the discussions too much. It took me about seven years of teaching to realize they were right. What better way to give up my control of a discussion than to have a student take control and be responsible for leading the discussion? As much as I hate to admit it, many times the discussions have been better when the students led them. It has been a humbling experience for me.

Often when I try a new exercise or project in class, I have several objectives in mind. In the writing exercise, for instance, I want the students to learn more about writing and also to learn more about giving and receiving feedback. With the discussion leaders project, I want the students to have a more open, free-flowing discussion, and I want them to learn what it is like when you are responsible for getting other people to talk—when you are trying to bring out other people's ideas and not your own.

This exercise is not the same thing as running a meeting. It's more like running a brain-storming session, where you are trying to get participants to express their ideas. I had discovered when I was in business that when I ran a meeting (was chairman) I tended to dominate all the participants. I already knew the outcome I wanted and the participants sensed this. They would not offer new ideas because they felt that I would not be receptive to them, since I had already made up my mind. Besides, my body language tangibly indicated my irritation at anything that kept us from moving the agenda along as quickly as possible.

Over the years I have worked hard to change my approach—especially as it applies to teaching. Of course, it depends on the type of meeting. I am talking about the kind of meeting where the object is to generate new ideas, new approaches, new insights. What the leader must do in this kind of meeting is to create a climate where all participants feel free to express themselves and are encouraged to do so. At this stage, the leader must make sure that all views are respected, that speakers are not judged or made to feel they are incorrect or ignorant, and that no one is allowed to dominate the discussion. It is a tall order.

I appoint two discussion leaders to an assigned article or book. The reason for two is largely logistic; we don't have enough time for everyone to be a solo discussion leader. The job of these leaders is to generate thinking and discussion about the reading. They are not to analyze or outline the reading. They must do what is necessary to get others to share their views about it. Good leaders bring the best out of their followers. Good discussion leaders bring the best out of the participants.

There are some advantages to having two people responsible for leading the discussion. One of them can act as an observer and help get the discussion back on track if the class has gone off on a tangent. He or she can also observe the body language of the participants. It's amazing the number of times participants want to speak, but the discussion leader does not notice them because he or she is too busy talking. The two can also help each other out if they get stuck.

I am still learning about this exercise. The tendency of a number of students—and executives—is to talk too much. They want to give their opinion and analysis. A large number of the male executives I have worked with make this mistake. When they hear the word "leader," they immediately think of taking control and taking charge. The problem is that it doesn't work. I point out that their job is to get the others talking. They can't do this if they themselves are talking.

One of the best ways of generating discussion is through questions, but the leaders must be careful of the kinds of questions they ask. You don't want to put participants on the defensive (the way most professors do—thus killing discussions) by asking a question that has just a right or wrong answer. Instead, the question should involve something participants can relate to based on their own experience.

Discussion leaders must listen to participants. So many of us concentrate on what we want to say. We have a preconceived notion of how the discussion should proceed, and through our control we actually cut off the discussion. Most students find this exercise helpful, but a number of them feel I should do a better job explaining what I mean by discussion leader. When they see the word *leader*, they immediately think they must take over and do all the work themselves. I need to do a better job of instructing them ahead of time.

And I definitely need to do a better job of providing a review at the end of each class. I need to ask them questions to get them thinking about the process—what works and what doesn't. This is something I know intellectually, but I fail to do it time after time. My excuse is always a lack of time. That simply is not a valid excuse. The best way to get the most from the exercise is to ask students what they discovered from doing it—while it is still fresh in everybody's mind. The subsequent discussion with suggestions and observations from all the participants creates the opportunity for real learning. You not only need to practice the behavior, you need to observe the process and learn what works and what doesn't and why. Then you know what you must work on to become more effective next time.

21.

Ethics

We only learn what we always knew.
—Marilyn Ferguson

A lot of business schools around the country have become concerned with teaching ethics. Can you teach ethics? I come up with the same answer as I do to the question, can you teach leadership? Technically, the answer is no. You can't teach ethics or leadership to someone else. You can create an environment where students can learn about ethics and leadership, but I don't think you can teach them to be ethical or to be leaders. They must learn how through their own experience.

Ultimately your ethical values are reflected in your behavior. It's not what you say; it's what you do. Reading what Plato or Aristotle said is one thing. How you react when you must make a choice that will affect someone else is another. I think a lot of us are afraid to "teach" ethics because we are not comfortable with ourselves and our own values. That is where it starts. Students quickly figure out the teacher's ethical values. They just observe the teacher's actions and especially how he or she treats the students. It's impossible to get across a credible message about treating people fairly when you don't even show these people respect in your everyday interaction with them.

I maintain that every one of my class sessions is about ethics. Ethics is not something you can effectively isolate and study separately. I don't think a business school has made much of a difference by requiring students to take a course in business ethics. That's part of the immunization theory of education: "I had English 101, and I had Business Ethics, and therefore I am educated and know all I need to about English and about ethics." We should recognize that we are teaching something about ethics every time we go into a class.

I am not arguing that we should eliminate courses in ethics. Certainly we should expose students to studies in ethics, and with all these reservations, I still devote an entire class to ethics. I share my concerns about teaching ethics and point out that there is still great value in reading different points of view and discussing the issues openly. Such reading and discussion help the students determine how they want to behave when they have to make tough choices.

For the seventh class session the students read six articles. I assign a pair of discussion leaders for each article. The whole class period is devoted to discussions of the articles. The six articles are:

- "Managers and Lovers" by Eliza G. C. Collins;
- "The Interrelationship of Ethics and Power in Today's Organizations" by Charles M. Kelly;
- "Ethical Managers Make Their Own Rules" by Sir Adrian Cadbury;
- "Letter from Birmingham City Jail" by Martin Luther King, Jr.;
- "The Nobel Evening Address" by the Dalai Lama;

• Chief Seattle's Speech

We cover the first three articles in the first half of the class. "Managers and Lovers" was published in 1983 and can still generate heated discussions. Some students think the article is dated and no longer relevant, and others think it is right on the money. Discussions usually take us into the world of vastly different corporate cultures. Many of my students (particularly the undergraduates) have worked for UPS, a company which forbids a supervisor from dating another employee and forbids the hiring of relatives of any employee. This policy contrasts with that of Brown-Forman, where planned nepotism and the laws of primogeniture prevail, and of the University of Louisville, where lots of married couples are employed. Which is right? We don't come up with one right answer, but we do recognize some of the ethical difficulties of trying to control employees' behavior on the one hand, and having no policy on the other. When managers become lovers, there are going to be problems. How do we deal with them?

In "Ethics and Power," Charles Kelly describes a certain kind of leader as a "Destructive Achiever." This is a difficult article for some students who have had limited business experience—they just don't know what he is talking about. But for those who have ever worked for a Destructive Achiever, this is an eye-opening analysis. Kelly describes the kind of leader that Jack Welch of GE says is "the most difficult for many of us to deal with. That leader delivers commitments, makes all the numbers, but doesn't share the values we must have. This is the individual who typically forces performance out of people rather than inspires it: the autocrat, the big shot, the tyrant." Welch says that GE can no longer afford to put up with this type of manager. Yet this is the kind of manager who gets results, particularly short-term results in a turn-around situation. What is the balance between getting the job done now—at all human costs—and developing people for the long term?

Sir Adrian Cadbury's "Ethical Managers" is one of the best articles I have read on business ethics. Sir Adrian clearly states the fundamentals. He says that what matters most is "where we stand as individual managers and how we behave when faced with decisions that require us to combine ethical and commercial judgments." We must first determine what our personal rules of conduct are (where is the line we won't cross?), and then we must think through who else will be affected by our decision. If everyone in a responsible business position followed this advice, we could save not only a lot of grief and worry, but also a lot of lawyers' fees.

My favorite sentence in the article is, "Our ethics are expressed in our actions, which is why they are usually clearer to others than to ourselves."

After the break we discuss the last three articles. Reading and discussing King's letter is a deeply moving experience. To me, this is one of the great documents in our American heritage, and yet the majority of my students has never read it before. More amazing to me, a number of my African-American students have not read it either. King's letter is a shock to my younger students. Many of them were born in the late 60s, and they had no idea that the kinds of things King describes were taking place in their lifetimes. These students cannot understand the point of view of the eight Alabama clergymen, whose statement inspired King's letter. They just don't see how religious leaders could have held these views. Sometimes we are wiser in hindsight.

My experience has been that it is easy for the discussion of King's letter to get off track. He is dealing with highly emotional issues, and a student's story or recollection can trigger all kinds of thoughts—and off we go. I have been using King's letter for about eight years, and what impresses me about the students' reaction to it is their overwhelming good will and respect for each other's views and their sadness about racial prejudice and discrimination. King's letter makes us all think about who we are and the values we live by.

The letter is remarkable. It is one of the finest examples I have ever come across of ethos, pathos, and logos in a written document. King's use of metaphor is masterful and reminds me of Lincoln. The imagery is familiar but his usage is hauntingly powerful. King says, "Nonviolence demands that the means we use must be as pure as the ends we seek." What a marvelous juxtaposition to *The Prince*, which the students read the following week. In short, I tell the students, "If any of you can write as beautifully as Martin Luther King, you can write more than one page." No one has tried to take me up on that.

We go from King's letter to the Dalai Lama's Nobel Evening Address. I unabashedly admire the Dalai Lama and consider him one of the great spiritual leaders that I am proud to look up to, and I was thrilled when he won the Nobel Peace Prize in 1989. One of the highlights of my life was being in the same room with him and hearing him in person when he came to Louisville in 1994. He is a holy man. I wanted to give my students some exposure to him, and I have used both his Nobel Evening Address and the Nobel Peace Prize Lecture. Both express his philosophy, simply and elegantly.

If you believe that a person's ethics are expressed in his behavior, then the Dalai Lama is one of the most ethical people on this planet. He bears no anger or hatred toward the Chinese, even though they have driven him and his people from their homeland, and are destroying Tibet, its culture, and its citizens. How well he lives up to the Christian ideal to love your enemies.

The Dalai Lama's message is so simple and straightforward that some students find difficulty with it. They think there must be some hidden message they are not getting. The discussions of the Dalai Lama's talk are uneven. Some have been stimulating, and some have been plodding and grasping for substance. One of the more interesting discussions took place when a young student asked what kind of president of UPS we thought the Dalai Lama would make!

Part of the reason for this difficulty is that this discussion comes towards the end of the class. The students are tired. But the other problem is that a number of students just don't see the relevance of what the Dalai Lama is saying to their own lives. I think that they just have not lived enough yet. They eventually will see it. But in the meantime, the Dalai Lama gives them plenty to think about regarding ethics—and some questions to ask themselves, such as what kind of life do you want to live and how do you want to relate to your fellow human beings?

The Dalai Lama's message is that we should live with compassion and kindness toward all sentient beings and in harmony with nature. We cannot continue to exploit our natural resources and damage our ecosystems. This philosophy is a perfect introduction to Chief Seattle's speech. I don't appoint discussion leaders for the speech. Instead I play a videotape of Joseph Campbell reading the speech on Bill Moyers' program, *The Power of Myth*.

The students love the video. Many are palpably moved by it, and angry at how we have abused the land and our natural resources—and how we have mistreated Native Americans. I then say, " I have an ethical problem. There is a question about the authenticity of Chief Seattle's speech. It's doubtful that he ever said those words—even though they have been immortalized in the popular children's book, *Brother Eagle, Sister Sky: A Message from Chief Seattle*. So, is it ethical for me to assign you a reading that may be bogus?"

We have a thoughtful discussion. Most students are too polite to say that I am not ethical. They say that it is all right to assign the article because it contains a message that they should hear. It contributes to our discussion of ethical principles and how we should live. I would be unethical, however, if I failed to disclose my knowledge that the speech might not be authentic. To my students, my disclosure takes me off the hook. Openness, it seems to me, is a significant aspect of ethical behavior. This is just a small example.

In concluding our discussion, I share with the students a couple of my favorite quotations from the Dalai Lama. Back in 1979 in San Francisco he talked about the problem of modern man and the environment. In one sentence he summed up the essence of what has been happening ecologically more brilliantly than any scientist I am aware of:

> When man changes the environment too quickly, say, for example, by burning the oceans of oil in the earth's crust and turning them into a gas in the earth's atmosphere, he creates a situation in which the environment then changes at a rate faster than his own rate of adaptation.

In *Kindness, Clarity, and Insight* he said,

> In Sanskrit, the word "ethics" is *shila* which is etymologized as meaning "attainment of coolness." When persons possess ethics, their minds have a peacefulness or coolness free from the heat of regretting what they have done.

What a splendid definition of ethics.

> Treat the Earth well. It was not given to you by your parents. It was lent to you by your children.
> —African Proverb

22.

Résumé and Interview

From the outset I have included a special project: cover letter, résumé, and job interview.

At first I gave grades on each segment of the project, but I soon realized that what the students needed was honest feedback on their performance, not a grade. Besides, it was demeaning to get a C on your résumé. So I dropped the grading, and this made the project less of an academic exercise. At first my approach had been that the students would send me their final résumé, and I would grade it. Now I work with them ahead of time, if they wish, helping them to develop the most effective résumé they can.

In my first graduate classes, this exercise was optional. I felt that the graduate students were more set in their careers and didn't need as much help. I was wrong. Changes hit the marketplace, and people who thought they had a secure career found their jobs—or divisions—were being eliminated. Some of the people who thought that they would never have to be in the job interview game again, suddenly found they were in it. They needed help. So the exercise became mandatory for all students.

For the eighth class session, I ask the students to write me a cover letter asking for a job interview. They can use whatever name, title, and organization they want. I want the exercise to be as realistic for them as possible. They enclose their résumé with the cover letter. We set appointments, and they meet with me in my office for the interview. They bring their cassettes with them to the interview, and we videotape it. I then give them feedback on their letter, résumé, and interview.

There is no esoteric, pedagogical reason I do the résumé project at this time. My chief reason is for convenience. Since I don't assign a memo in conjunction with the articles on ethics, I find this a good time to do the résumé. This is also at the half-way point of the class, and I am able to give students more meaningful feedback since I have been observing them for some time.

Letter

I strongly urge the students to use a conversational style in their cover letter. The letter should have a positive tone and should flow smoothly. They should not over-sell. Sometimes students don't know the purpose of the letter. They think it is to get the job. I tell them that they don't know at this point if this is a job they want. The purpose of the letter is to get an interview. I suggest they put themselves in the shoes of the interviewer: "If you received this letter, would you want to interview the writer?"

Of course, I check out all the details. Typos, misspellings, and grammatical errors will just about assure that you won't be asked to the interview.

Résumé

The résumé is more difficult to evaluate. All I can do is give the students my honest reaction. I point out that everyone they talk to will give them a different suggestion on how to write a résumé. I tell them not to put anything in their résumé or take anything out, just because I suggested it. "It's your résumé and your career. You're the one who must be pleased with the résumé. You're the one who's going to have the interview—not me."

I have some views I share with the students. The problem with using a résumé writing program or service, which a number of undergraduates do, is that the formats of the résumés all look the same. If you are competing for a job, you want to stand out. Some people insist that an employment objective be listed at the top of the résumé. Most students hate what they have written, but have included it because they were told they had to. I find most of the objectives ludicrous and tell the students to take them out of the résumé—if they want to. The objective is either broad and vague: "Seeking a responsible position in a dynamic and progressive organization that can utilize my organizational, administrative, and leadership abilities," or it is specifically written for the job being offered: "Level 1 Computer Programmer." In both cases the objective is meaningless.

I recommend the elimination of the word *utilize*. This is the favorite word of canned résumé packages. It sounds pompous. I also recommend getting rid of adjectives. When students claim to have "excellent communication skills" on the résumé, but then have errors in their cover letter, or they interview poorly, their credibility is shot. "Excellent" is a matter of judgment. I advise against putting this kind of statement in the résumé. Just stick with those things that are factual—what you have done. And use verbs wherever you can.

You are trying to present as strong a picture of yourself as you can. Eliminate all padding.

I think it is a good idea to try to get your résumé on one page, but I am not a stickler for this any longer. If your experience justifies it, or if the position you are seeking requires it, then two pages are acceptable. But that's my limit.

Interview

Several years ago a student suggested that it would be helpful to make audio tapes of the interviews. I agreed and for a couple of years students brought tape recorders to the interview. I never listened to a tape, but the students told me the tapes were of great benefit to them. Then one day a student forgot her tape recorder, but had brought her video cassette instead. By this time I had my own camcorder, so we decided to videotape the interview. After she had reviewed the tape, she told the class that taping had been most helpful—that it was instructive to see her facial expressions and body language in answering the questions. From then on, we have videotaped all the interviews and now include my feedback on the tape, as well.

The interview I conduct is similar to interviews I did with prospective employees at my company. I don't ask technical questions. The applicant is not going to work directly for me. Most companies now conduct a series of interviews with candidates. My role is that of an executive of the company who is one of the interviewers. For many years I have used the interview to find out about a person's character and values, maturity, desires and motivation, sense of self-acceptance, and to determine whether I wanted him or her on my team. This is the kind of interview I conduct with my students. These are the questions I ask:

1. **Education**. Why are you getting an MBA? or Why did you choose your major?

2. **Goals/Future**. What do you want to be doing in five years? What would be an ideal job for you?

3. **Accomplishment/Achievement**. What accomplishment or achievement are you proudest of? What has given you the greatest satisfaction?

4. **Experience/Learning**. What have you learned from your present (previous) job?

5. **Qualification**. Why should I hire you? What do you bring to the job?

6. **References**. What would your references say about you?

7. **Interests**. What do you like to do for enjoyment in your "spare" time?

8. **Imagination/Dream**. Hypothetical question: You have all the money you need and you are given the gift of some free time with no obligations to anyone. Under those circumstances, what would you do for fun for yourself?

9. **Curiosity**. What would be the questions you would ask if this were a real interview?

10. **Values**. When you think about your life, and deep down what's really important to you, what is it?

I then have one last question, "What question that I did not ask you, do you wish that I had asked?" This is usually unexpected, and students can see how they deal with the unexpected. With the exception of this last one, all the questions were ones I asked in interviews I conducted in my business.

A point I stress is asking questions. I remind students that the interview is two-way. The student is also interviewing the company (or the company's representatives) to find out if this is where he or she wants to work. A number of interviewers now judge the quality of the candidates by the questions they ask. We frequently hear, "I think Mary is exactly who we are looking for. She asked all the right questions."

From my point of view, there is a lot of misinformation in the marketplace regarding how to interview for a job. A lot of advice is not helpful. In fact, it is harmful. I urge the students to be as natural as they can and to answer the questions honestly. This does not mean the interview is a confessional. But it does mean the student should avoid canned answers and phony techniques. You must be yourself. Any competent interviewer will see right through pretensions.

I tell the students, "Suppose you fool the interviewer by answering the questions, not honestly, but by giving the answer the interviewer wants. Say you get hired. Then the real you shows up on the job. This turns out not to be the person the company thought it was hiring. You and the company are incompatible; you must go. It's not worth it. You have gained nothing. Be honest. Be yourself. If the company doesn't like you, then this is not the place for you."

The problem is, there is so much pressure to get a job— any job. But taking the first job offer that comes along is like marrying the first person you date. It might work, but the odds are stacked against you. The best advice on career planning is Richard Nelson Bolles's *What Color Is Your Parachute?* Several former students recommended it to me, and I now recommend it to those students who are trying to decide on their careers. So many of my students feel guilty because they don't know what they want to do. I think they feel a little better when I tell them that I don't know many fifty-year-olds who really know what they want to do, either.

Overwhelmingly, students say that this exercise—particularly the résumé and interview—is helpful to them. But the interview is a bit awkward for some students. Some have a problem with role playing, and some have no idea what they want to do. If you don't know what you want to do—what kind of career or work you want—it is hard to pull off a good interview. After all, you are selling yourself in an interview. If you don't know what you want, you don't know what to sell.

A few students think it is too easy interviewing with me—they feel too comfortable. They say that I don't ask tough enough questions. However, we usually end up agreeing that *I* have to feel comfortable in the interview. If I try to be someone else, I won't be authentic, and the whole exercise will be less meaningful to them.

The interviews are fun for me. They allow me to get to know my students better. I have conducted more than 600 interviews since I have been teaching, and sometimes I get a real surprise.

I was going through an interview with a student who was in his late twenties. He was married and had a couple of children he was proud of. He lived in a small town, some miles outside of Louisville, and was a hard worker with strong values. I knew all this about him, but was totally unprepared for his answer to the question: "What accomplishment or achievement are you proudest of?"

With almost no hesitation he replied, "That I was a good son to my father."

His answer took my breath away. I had never gotten a response like that. He went on, "My mother died when I was twelve and my brother was ten. My father raised us. He sacrificed everything for us and devoted his life to us. He was the best father a son could have. He got cancer a couple of years ago, and I moved back to take care of him in the last months before he died. I'm glad that I could do something for him; he had done so much for me. That's what I am proudest of—that I was a good son to my father."

Another response that stands out in my memory is that of an older man, probably in his mid-forties. He was getting his doctorate in education. He had grown up in South Chicago, the youngest of thirteen children. His father had abandoned the family, and his mother had raised him and most of his siblings by herself. I asked him, "When you think about your life, and deep down what is really important to you, what is it?"

After a long pause, he said quite softly, "That I say 'thank you' to my mother." Then the tears welled up in his eyes and began to roll down his cheeks.

Through his tears he said, "I am so fortunate to be where I am. I never dreamed I could get a doctoral degree. So many people have helped me, but most of all my mother. She always believed in me and supported me. She would be so proud of me now. She died last year. I hope she knows how much I thank her. I think she does."

A woman in her late thirties answered the question, what was important to her, without any hesitation: "To be a good mother, a good wife, and a good daughter—in that order." Now that's having your priorities straight!

These were moving moments for me. I feel honored that the students have shared them with me. They taught me something about values, something about timeless values, way beyond any class in business school: honor thy father and thy mother. These students had done that. I had a lot to learn from them. No wonder I have so much respect for my students.

23.

Questions

Always the beautiful answer that
asks a more beautiful question.
—e. e. cummings

After I had been teaching for a few years, I began to understand the importance of asking questions. When you think about it, you realize that one of the principal ways we learn is by asking questions. Yet most of us have never had any instruction in how to ask questions. It's amazingly the same situation as we have with listening. We get no training; we are just expected to know how to do it.

For many students their experience in the classroom has discouraged them from asking questions. They are rewarded for giving answers, and especially answers to the teacher's questions, exactly as the teacher wants the answer. This kind of activity might foster memorization, but it does little to promote either real thinking or real learning. I think teachers should spend more time helping students to articulate the urgent questions than demanding right answers. I believe that thinking starts with a question. If students are going to learn to think, then they have to learn to ask questions.

Asking questions is a behavior. We learn it by doing it. One of the opportunities I give the students to ask questions is with the guests who come to the class. These guests come to most of the classes in the last half of the semester. I ask the guests to talk for about 15 minutes about how they got where they are and the values that are important to them. Then the students take over for the next hour with their questions.

Before we start having sessions with the guests, I give the students a one-page handout on questions that I wrote several years ago (see Appendix IV). The handout serves as a focus for us as we discuss the importance of asking questions and try to discover what determines a good question.

My thinking has been stimulated by the thoughts of Neil Postman and Charles Weingartner in *Teaching as a Subversive Activity*:

> Once you have learned how to ask questions—relevant and appropriate and substantial questions—you have learned how to learn and no one can keep you from learning whatever you want or need to know.... The most important intellectual ability man has yet developed—the art and science of asking questions—is not taught in school.

Asking questions also has a lot to do with creativity. Creative people always question things. They are curious and this curiosity feeds their imagination. One of the complaints about formal schooling is that it stifles creativity in the students. Our creativity begins with a question. Antony Jay says, "The uncreative mind can spot wrong answers, but it takes the creative mind to spot wrong questions."

I think that asking the right questions is a significant part of leadership. After all, CEOs of large corporations can't go around telling people what to do. They can't know everything and they certainly haven't got all the answers. But they can exercise leadership through their questions. These questions send messages to the people involved and help them focus on the right objectives. Asking questions becomes a sophisticated form of delegation and development of others—it causes others to think for themselves.

Nowhere is the need to ask questions more obvious than in the corporate board meeting. How often do directors come out of a meeting looking puzzled, giving each other confused looks, and feeling that they have been fed a lot of meaningless data? They complain and ask each other, "What's going on?"—but they remained silent during the meeting. They are often afraid to ask the dumb question for fear of looking dumb themselves. At times the dumb question needs to be asked, and I have found that the strong, effective leaders are usually the ones with enough self-confidence to ask it.

It takes courage to ask dumb questions in public. What is a "dumb" question? Basically it is simple, to the point, and open-ended. You ask it because you don't know the answer but would like to. You genuinely want to hear the other person's response. It's a good idea to keep your question brief. If you hide your question in a long, opinionated statement, you put the other person on the defensive. What you want is an honest response, and a brief, concise question is more likely to get it.

I tell the students to ask our guests any questions they are curious about. That always makes a good question. Never ask a question in order to impress someone else. Don't be afraid to ask personal questions. I have found that personal questions have sometimes produced the most revealing and meaningful responses.

I want the students to take the opportunity with our guests to find out what they want to know. The way to do this is by asking questions.

The more comfortable students become in asking questions of guests, the better they get and the more self-confidence they gain. They can carry over this competence and confidence as they participate in meetings at work. Effective participants in meetings ask good questions.

> *Learning begins with questions we cannot answer;*
> *it ends with questions we can.*
>
> —Russell Ackoff

24.

Guests

Right from the beginning, I knew that I wanted to emphasize practical aspects of leadership in my class. One thing I could do for my students that they could not do for themselves was to give them the opportunity to meet and interact with leaders from the Louisville community.

I now bring into the class six guests. I try to give the students a variety in age, experience, position, gender, race, and type of organization—whether for-profit or not-for-profit, or large or small. Lining up the guests I want—when I want them—is a challenge. They have difficult schedules to work with. They love to come to the class; it's fun and stimulating to respond to the students' questions.

Ideally in a semester I would have an entrepreneur, the head of a government agency or a not-for-profit organization, the CEO of a major corporation, the president of a smaller company or the head of a division of a larger company, a venture capitalist or someone in a service business, and the President of the University of Louisville. Some guests have come to the class a number of times. I try to be careful about wearing out the welcome mat. I am grateful to all of them. They provide an extraordinary opportunity for the students to learn.

I ask the guests to talk for about 15 minutes about their own career and what is important to them (their values) and to then answer students' questions.

Guests come at 5:30 and stay for a little over an hour. Some follow my instructions precisely; others talk too long. The most effective guests are generally those who are open about who they are and what is important to them. They answer questions thoughtfully and honestly, but briefly and to the point. Some guests have rambled and have used an answer to launch another ten-minute monologue. This is usually not effective because it means that students have less time to ask questions. I say "usually" because there are exceptions. Occasionally, a lengthy answer has been so brilliant and insightful that we have all learned from it. But most often, students can see the kind of communication that is effective—and it's not long-windedness.

Students can sense those guests who listen to them and to their questions and who show them respect. I can feel the students tune into them. On the other hand, I have had a few guests who were absorbed with themselves. They tended to lecture and to give the impression that they were superior to the students. I imagine they treat their employees the same way. Students are not fooled. Their reactions are clearly stated in their later remarks, "I would love to work for her," or "I would hate to work for him."

I can never tell how a class is going to react to a given guest. Some of the guests have come to the class several times. Sometimes the interaction of that guest with the class is fantastic—you can feel the electricity—and sometimes there is little energy or connection. Each class has its own personality. Sometimes it's the right question that opens up the guest. At other times, I have seen the same guest preoccupied, and the energy never gets flowing. But there is no such thing as a bad or a poor guest. The students always learn something valuable from each guest, and they tell me that the guests are one of the most valuable aspects of the class.

After they have met with several guests, the students begin to realize that there is no magic formula for successful leadership. Each of the guests seems to do it his or her own way. Few, if any, of them planned to be where they are now. Nearly all of them responded to some key opportunities in their lives. They took a risk and changed what they were doing, and that made a tremendous difference.

Some things that nearly all of the guests emphasize (in no particular order) are:

- A sense of integrity. If you don't have integrity, you won't last long.
- Hard work. Energy. A passion for what they are doing.
- Communications. An ability to communicate orally and in writing.
- Focus on priorities. You must know what is important, and you must stick to it.
- Failures. Hard times. You learn from your mistakes, and you don't give up.

Beyond these points, there is great variety. Some cannot work for someone else. They have their own companies. Some are splendid politicians and love playing the political game. Some are intellectual and some are street smart. Some have Ph.D.s and some have no college education. Some are extraordinarily good "people" persons. Some are tough taskmasters. Some love to make money. Some are more interested in their mission.

It really gets interesting when we get into the more personal questions. Most of the older males (more nearly my age) say that they should have had more balance in their lives when their children were younger. They urge the students to have more balance in their lives. When the students ask them how to do this, they usually answer, "I don't really know. But I should have done a better job."

"Yes, but if you had spent more time at home with your wife and children, would you have gotten where you are today?"

The answer: a sheepish "Probably not."

This illustrates a dilemma the students face. They want meaningful, productive business careers, but they also want a wholesome family life. The two often conflict. The problem for the women students is even greater. This is the first generation that has wanted both motherhood and a business career. It's difficult at best, and our women guests get grilled on this subject. Their answers are thoughtful and helpful, but it is clear that there are no magic answers. You have to figure out what works best for you.

What it finally gets down to, it seems to me, is that individuals must know themselves, their values, and what is important to them. They then must do their best to live their lives accordingly. The important thing is to examine your life and to determine who you want to be and how you are going to live.

Many of my students are surprised at how well they can relate to the experience of many of the guests. The students are surprised to learn how many of the guests started out with nothing—in the way of material wealth. A number of them worked their way through college and worked second jobs to support their family in the early years of their marriage. The students get a different impression from the fat-cat CEO they had expected. Instead, they see a hard-working, down-to-earth human being who has gone through some tough times, who is decent, who has a fine sense of humor, who loves his or her family, and who readily gives credit to others, to timing, and to luck.

There have been many magical moments with the guests. Here are some highlights.

Margaret Greene on several occasions has been a guest when we were discussing *The Prince*. Margaret was a political science major as an undergraduate and can still quote Machiavelli. As President of BellSouth, Kentucky, she had been responsible for several corporate downsizings. Machiavelli becomes totally relevant when Margaret talks about her challenge in determining whether it is better to be loved or feared.

The students also see that her two young children are a priority in her life. She manages to keep that priority while giving her organization the leadership it needs. She does all this with a fine sense of perspective and sense of humor, without taking herself too seriously. No wonder the students see her as an inspiring role model.

Ed Abrain has been to my class twice. He was President of the PowerBuilt Golf division of Hillerich & Bradsby and has had lots of marketing experience. Ed shared a technique he has used in marketing that I found fascinating: "Describe a product or service in terms of a person. Male or female, young or old, exciting or dull, glitzy or solid, tame or wild." Ed pointed out that this was fairly easy to do with a car. For instance, a Cadillac is about 65 years old, solid, dependable, expensive, and a bit stodgy. A BMW is about 30 years old, powerful, sporty, expensive, and a performer. Ed can give a precise personality to any brand of golf club on the market.

I wonder about my class. I'd like to say it is young, vigorous, still growing, still learning, curious, exciting, and vital. What about your organization? How would you describe it?

David Grissom is always willing to come to my class. He is currently Chairman of Mayfair Capital and was formerly

CEO of Citizens Fidelity Bank. David and I have been on corporate boards together for over 25 years. We were on each other's board—what is now pejoratively called an interlocking directorship. I consider David one of the most effective board members I have served with.

David is a terrific guest. He is interested in the students and is open with them and candid in his responses. He knows a lot about business and does not beat around the bush. He exudes energy and drive, but it is the human element that the students ultimately connect with.

They are surprised that he worked his way through college and law school, that he started his law practice on borrowed money, that he taught classes at night at U of L to supplement his income. Some students are under the impression that all successful bankers started out rich. It doesn't always work that way.

Some of the students are familiar with David's son, David, who is an accomplished jazz guitarist having played to rave reviews in Carnegie Hall as lead guitarist with John Cougar Mellancamp's group. They are surprised at the supportive relationship David has with his son, who went in an entirely different direction than he did. When they learn that David's first wife died as a result of an automobile accident when she was 30, leaving him with three young children to raise, they begin to understand that the important things in life—even for a successful, hard-driving businessman—are deeply held values and strong family relationships. Character counts.

Joan Riehm was Deputy Mayor of the City of Louisville. She was one of the best participants we have had in the Effective Executive program, and she has come to my classes for a number of years. Joan is a fabulous communicator and knows how to connect with the students. She is especially good in talking about careers and how to make career choices. "First, figure out what you like to do. Then determine what you are good at. And then decide what you really care about.

If you can combine these three things, you can make more sensible career decisions."

On several occasions Joan has shared her father's adage to her: "It's not who you know; it's who knows you." She makes a strong pitch for the students to get involved in volunteer organizations. That's one way people can get to know you. Joan is a splendid example of the capable, dedicated public servant, and she demonstrates to the students the importance of the whole community, and not just the business community.

David Jones is a legend in Louisville. He founded Humana and is undoubtedly Louisville's best known businessperson. David and I are contemporaries, and for a while he served on my company's board of directors. I was looking for someone who was independent. I found him!

He has been a guest in my class four of five times. Each time is a highlight for the students. Many of my students have been employees of Humana. It is a special treat to sit down with the founder—someone they have heard so much about—and just have a pleasant conversation.

David is remarkable. There are not many people out there who founded a company and are still CEO some 30 years later when the company has over $3.5 billion in sales and over 4,000 employees. He is extremely disciplined and focused. And he knows his priorities. He is interested in young people, and he makes sure he balances his personal life and his business obligations.

David has a close relationship with Peter Drucker. He is founding chair of the Peter F. Drucker Graduate Management Center's Board of Visitors in Claremont, California. Drucker was influential in helping David and the late Wendell Cherry set the strategic direction for Humana. I always get David to tell us about Peter Drucker, and his stories are fascinating.

The last time David came to the class a student asked

him about Wendell Cherry. It was moving to hear him describe his unique relationship with Wendell, and how Wendell was his closest friend and how much he missed him. "Wendell's death has left a hole in my heart." Who could possibly think that a successful businessperson has no heart?

Roger Hale is CEO of LG&E Energy. I serve on his board and was on the board when we hired him in 1989. He is a dynamic leader and one of the best CEOs I have ever been associated with. He has come to my class several times, and in his visit in 1995 he shared his views of leadership with the class. I've never seen my students take notes the way they did when he gave them his *Ten Principles for Effective Leadership*:

1. Be the world's best subordinate! Never bring a problem to the boss without a solution. Never say it's not my job. Never miss a deadline. Say it on one page. Anticipate requests. Remember, change always happens! Always give credit to others.

2. Learn how to pick the very best people—never compromise on people quality.

3. There is never a substitute or compromise on personal integrity. Set the highest standards—expect others to meet or exceed them. Being trusted is essential.

4. Always provide your subordinates with constant, informal feedback on issues/performance—constructive coaching. Never wait until year-end. It will mean less and generally doesn't go well. Never correct or get mad at a subordinate in front of a group—always do your coaching in private.

5. Remember, in any job you must always satisfy customers, employees, and shareholders. Make sure you give personal time to each group.

6. Develop a tolerance for and understanding of ambiguity—it will be a part of almost every management decision

you make.

7. Always find a way to get involved in the community in which you work—they deserve it, it's good development for you, and it helps the company or business image.

8. Read *In Search of Excellence.* The companies are dated, but the principles are right on target.

9. Always help other people network for jobs—inside and out—what goes around comes around!

10. Remember that failure is never final, and success is never certain.

He followed these up with *Seven Personal Principles for an Effective Work Life*:

1. Always take your vacation and occasional long weekends. To do otherwise is foolish and gets no points in and of itself.

2. Buy clothes that will last a long time. Always dress for work as if each day means something—you only get one chance to make a first impression.

3. Always stay in good physical shape. It says a lot for your character and you will perform better at everything.

4. Cultivate a good sense of humor—use it wisely and often—but always for the positive.

5. Always get to work early. A great start to the day and you get more accomplished than staying late. It's results that count—not effort.

6. Always carry a personal calendar and a note pad. Good ideas and the need to reschedule happen often.

7. You will never regret spending too much time with your children.

The students could have kept him there all night—and no wonder!

Bruce Lunsford is CEO of Vencor, one of Louisville's

fastest growing companies. Bruce has received all kinds of national recognition as an outstanding entrepreneur and businessperson and has even appeared on the cover of *Forbes* magazine. It's exciting when he comes into the classroom.

Through the Effective Executive program, I have worked with most of Vencor's top executives. These are all members of a team that Bruce has put together. They are a remarkable group. I have never come across such a diverse group of executives in any other organization. Bruce believes in diversity. It is a way of life in his company, and it pays off in performance. It is exciting to hear him talk about his people. He demands high performance and excellence. But at the same time he cares deeply about each individual. It's tough love in action. Bruce's enthusiasm is contagious. His energy lights up the room. The students are transfixed; they see what it takes to run a company and make it successful. It's people, but people with a passion and a commitment.

When one of the students asked Bruce where he had learned his important lessons, he said, "From my mother. She was my best friend. When she was killed in an automobile accident, it was the biggest loss in my life." And when another student asked him about the driving force in Vencor, he replied, "Well, a company has to have a heart."

No text book contains the wisdom these guests—and all the others—have shared with the students. The guests give the students a unique opportunity to learn what they need to know. They have been marvelous teachers.

And speaking of teachers, most of the guests mention the importance of teachers or mentors in their lives. At some stage in their development they were helped by a mentor, and now many of them serve as mentors to younger people.

Students are interested in the role of mentors. When they asked me if I ever had a mentor, I would answer, "No," and explain that in my business career I had largely found my own way. No one took me under his wing and gave me coaching and guidance.

But as I began thinking more deeply about my life—and my views about leadership—I realized I did have a mentor in my early life. His name is Charles Stanwood, and he has had a profound influence on me, on what I stand for, and on the kind of life I wish to lead.

Charlie is now retired and was director of Camp Pasquaney for many years. Pasquaney, a summer camp for boys is on New Found Lake in New Hampshire, and was founded in 1895. It is the oldest, continually-operated boys' camp in America. I went there as a boy and then in my late teens and early twenties as a counsellor.

Under Charlie's tutelage, I learned that the important aspects of leadership are character and integrity, dedication and commitment to something bigger than yourself, the urge to create and contribute, the self-discipline to achieve excellence and expertness, and the understanding and practice of what it takes to be a good follower. I also began to learn the importance of community. Leaders build a sense of community, no matter what the organization—a business corporation or a not-for-profit organization. With the proper leadership a sense of community is built in any institution, including the boardroom and the classroom. Leadership always functions within the framework of community.

As a further tribute to Charlie, his successor, John Gemmill, has been an outstanding director. I have worked intimately with John for the past twenty years, and I consider him one of the best leaders and executives I know. Part of being an effective leader is developing your successor. Charlie did that with John.

In *A World of Ideas II*, Bill Moyers has an interview with the poet Robert Bly. They discuss male initiators, men who care about the soul of a young man. This initiator blesses young men, and they point out that young men are in great need of this blessing. "Many boys don't know a single older man who encourages them, or who holds them in his heart."

When I was young, I had a male initiator in Charlie Stanwood. It made a tremendous difference in my development and self-confidence. Deep within my subconscious has been a strong desire to give back to other young people the "gift" I received from Charlie. I think both young men and young women need this kind of affirmation, and I have gladly given it where I could. This is my motivation, what I want to do as a teacher.

25.

The Prince

We are much beholden to Machiavel and others,
that write what men do, and not what they ought to do.
—Francis Bacon

In a course on leadership, it is just about impossible to avoid *The Prince*. Machiavelli's book is the classic on what is "useful" in exercising leadership. I maintain that I want my course to be practical, useful. That is also Machiavelli's aim. He is interested in what actually works in the real world and not some imagined theory that ought to work.

I am intrigued with *The Prince*. It was written nearly 500 years ago and still has the power to shock us. It hits close to home. All you have to do is to think about what has taken place in the world during the twentieth century. We may deplore what Machiavelli recommends, but we cannot deny that the leaders of many states and nations practice what he preaches.

Machiavelli wanted a strong leader for Florence who

would keep its citizens secure against its enemies. To maintain this security, the leader (the prince) would have to exercise power effectively. The leader's effectiveness would be judged solely by the results. It did not matter by what means these results were obtained. The ends justified the means.

To help the students get a better perspective on *The Prince*, I have them read the Introduction and first chapters of Antony Jay's *Management and Machiavelli*, the book that they read right after *The Prince*. Jay helps them see the relevance of *The Prince* to today's business world.

Although a few of my students like *The Prince*, the majority of them hate it. They don't like what Machiavelli is advocating. They think it is wrong to break your word or to rule by fear. Machiavelli's philosophy is the exact opposite of that espoused by Martin Luther King and the Dalai Lama—works that the students read the previous week.

How should a leader exercise power? Especially when confronted with an enemy who threatens your state (your organization) and who does not play by your ethical rules? These are questions that trouble me, and I don't have a satisfactory answer. Every time I get carried away by the teachings of Gandhi, King, and the Dalai Lama, I am slapped in the face by Machiavelli's vision of reality. We simply cannot deny that in the world of action, of politics, a lot of what Machiavelli says has merit. It works. The question is, for how long? Machiavelli deals with the short-term, with immediate results. Spiritual leaders deal with the long-term. But if you don't deal with the short-term, you may not survive for the long-term.

"The fact is that a man who wants to act virtuously in every way necessarily comes to grief among so many who are not virtuous." What a perfect description of Jimmy Carter's presidency. Most people would agree that Carter is a virtuous man who tries his best to lead a virtuous life. They would also agree that he was an ineffective President. He did not know how to exercise power—"how not to be virtuous"—to get desired results.

I think there is a dichotomy in leadership—between "spiritual" leaders and "political" leaders. Spiritual leaders appeal to ethical and spiritual values that are espoused in all major religions. Political leaders—including most business leaders—must make tough decisions to preserve the security of the nation—or the survival of the business. Their decisions and actions are sometimes in conflict with the ethical values of the spiritual leaders. The reality is that sometimes the ends do justify the means, and I find that reality difficult to deal with.

A good example, I think, is President Truman's decision to drop the atomic bomb on Japan in 1945. There is no doubt in my mind that based on the circumstances at the time, Truman did the right thing. He saved countless American and Japanese lives. But the debate about the ethics of his decision is still going on fifty years later.

While admitting that I have been influenced by David McCullough's superb biography, *Truman*, I still think that of all U.S. presidents in my lifetime, Truman comes closest to maintaining both high ethical standards while making tough political decisions. He knew how to exercise power, but he also knew what was right. He had extremely low popularity ratings at the time, but he did not pander to the pollsters. He was determined to do what was right for the country, and he did it. What a far cry from our contemporary political leaders, who must see what the polls say before they will take a stand or make a move.

In his introduction to *Nicholas and Alexandra*, Robert Massie says, "The virtues which we admire in private life and profess in our religion become secondary qualities in our rulers. The test of greatness in tsars or presidents is not in their private lives or even in their good intentions, but in their deeds." This is what Machiavelli is saying, and I reluctantly have concluded that it is probably true.

My father was U.S. Senator from Kentucky for twelve years, and during the mid-sixties he was also National Chairman of the Republican party. My father had strong ethical values. He believed in doing what was right for the country, and he believed in the dignity of his fellow human beings. He was a decent man. But he had to get elected, he had to represent the interests of his constituents. His "job" was to further the interests of the Republican party and to get Republican candidates elected. He had to compromise. I am sure he said things and did things he was not proud of. Although he never specifically talked with me about these issues, I could sense his anguish. It makes me wonder, is there anyone left in politics who would "rather be right than President"?

My students have asked me why I did not get into politics. I never had the desire. I knew the choices politicians have to make, and I was uncomfortable in having to make them. I just did not want to be in a position where I had to do things that went against my values—what I believed in. That could also be why I am no longer in management and am now teaching. I guess I could not stand the heat, so I got out of the kitchen.

Once I had a class that was completely turned off by *The Prince*. They didn't like the book and saw no relevance in sixteenth century Italian politics. A guest to the rescue! Our guest was Wendy Heck, a vice president of LG&E, who had been a former student in the class and who had also participated in the Effective Executive program. So she had read *The Prince* twice. The students were fascinated when Wendy told them that she had recently been promoted and put in charge of a large department where she had not worked before and which needed reorganizing. She had gotten all kinds of advice as to how to proceed, most of the old-timers telling her to go slow, don't rock the boat, and study the territory. She told the students she recalled something she had read in this class—

it was advice in *The Prince*:

> So it should be noted that when he seizes a state the new
> ruler must determine all the injuries that he will need to
> inflict. He must inflict them once for all, and not have to
> renew them every day, and in that way he will be able to
> set men's minds at rest and win them over to him when he
> confers benefits. Whoever acts otherwise, either through
> timidity or bad advice, is always forced to have the knife
> ready in his hand and he can never depend on his subjects
> because they, suffering fresh and continuous violence, can
> never feel secure in regard to him.

She did not delay and procrastinate. She took decisive
action, made the changes that were needed, and gave the department the direction that had been lacking. No one would
accuse Wendy of being Machiavellian. But the students had a
different attitude toward *The Prince* after her explanation of
its value to her.

For their memos, I ask the students: "*The Prince*, your
organization, and you. Is there a conflict of values? Your
thoughts."

Sometimes the students are surprised by what they find.
I remember one student who said, "I loved *The Prince*. I like
power and *The Prince* is about power!" Here are excerpts
from her memo:

> Machiavelli's theories better describe my values than
> those of my organization, and I am surprised by this. I
> assumed that the corporate attitude toward power would be
> closer to Machiavelli's views. I agree with the author's
> thinking on the importance of laying a foundation for
> power, the necessity of using both good and evil in
> managing, and the wisdom of strategic planning even in
> the absence of the need to plan. In examining the ap-

proaches of my peers, I see managers who do not recognize or understand the power they possess, and I become frustrated with my company's haphazard management.

The theories described in *The Prince* make sense to me. Reading Machiavelli makes me appreciate how I operate, and makes me annoyed at the lack of direction my peers seem to have. Some of the author's tenets of leadership appear ruthless, yet their application in management works. The territorial nature of my company and my co-workers bothers me, and ethical managerial conflicts happen when territories and corporate values overwhelm individual managers, or when managers do not comprehend power.

I believe Antony Jay when he states "the wisdom of princes is at the disposal of managers," and I wish that the other managers in my company would avail themselves of this wisdom.

The Prince is also relevant to the not-for-profit organization. Here is an excerpt from another memo:

Machiavelli presents a unique picture. He assumes that the prince's purpose is to be successful, and then draws from actual practice clear examples of what others have done to be successful. He tells it exactly as he sees it. There is no attempt to suggest what should be—only a description of what actually works.

The longer I am in a leadership position, the more I realize that "the gulf between how one should live and how one does live" is indeed wide. As a leader of a church affiliated children's program, I am tempted to dwell on what should be. There are times when I succumb only to realize that my purpose is to lead an organization in the real world.

In the real world I have to live with both the church

and the state and keep both happy; I must constantly uphold the spiritual aspect when in reality that may be the problem. Like Machiavelli, I recognize the importance of appearances and results, and I have learned how to maintain appearances and find results when none are readily apparent.

There are many hard choices that I must make and several present ethical dilemmas. There is no one correct way, so in the end I must make a decision on what I believe is best for my organizations. That to me is what Machiavelli is saying in his presentation on virtues.

In March of 1988 an employee of Kentucky Fried Chicken had this perspective:

The Prince must have been required reading for the corporate planners at PepsiCo because the methods they employed when acquiring Kentucky Fried Chicken were strictly Machiavellian.

In the book, Machiavelli maintains that when states are newly acquired there are three basic ways to hold them:

1. By letting them keep their own laws, exacting tribute, and setting up an oligarchy which will keep them friendly to you.
2. By going and living there in person.
3. By devastating them.

Pepsi followed this advice to the letter. First, they assured KFC management that nothing would change under the new ownership. The rules and methods would stay the same and KFC would be allowed to operate as they always had.

Pepsi's next step was to transfer Pepsi executives into key positions within the KFC organization, including the

Senior VP of Marketing, the VP of Human Resources, and the VP of Finance.

Everyone thought it odd that the new Senior VP of Marketing chose to locate in the basement of Corporate headquarters rather than in the executive suite. But when black Friday came, we gained greater understanding of his tactics. On black Friday Machiavelli's third step was carried out. One by one, selected employees were summoned to the Senior VP's basement office and dismissed. At the end of the day, half of the Marketing staff had been let go.

Pepsi's acquisition was a painful experience. Their methods seemed cruel and thoughtless. However, now I realize that they were probably necessary to ensure their hold on us and our long term success.

In October 1988 an employee of Humana wrote this memo:

Recently the *Courier-Journal* ran several articles about Humana denying insurance coverage of a liver transplant for a critically ill man. Just yesterday, I heard a similar story about Humana denying coverage of an experimental cancer treatment for a man in Florida. I'm sure my initial reaction to these stories was the same as most people's. I wanted the company—my company—to change its position and help the unfortunate people out. I questioned how I could work for an organization that could not only ignore, but increase human suffering.

Reading *The Prince* changed my perspective. In *The Prince*, Machiavelli said, "There is nothing so self-defeating as generosity: in the act of practicing it, you lose the ability to do so..." When I first read this statement it made me angry. I like to think of myself as a generous person. By giving of myself, I am enriched, not lessened. After some thought, however, I realized Machiavelli was not talking about generosity of spirit, but generosity as it relates to material goods. In that respect, his statement is correct.

In a way, allowing the insurance coverage would have been the easy way out for Humana. This is especially true after the press got hold of the stories. The company could have saved itself some damaging publicity. The question is, how many of these exceptions could the company grant? The answer is, very few before either premium rates would have to be raised for all Humana Health Plan members or before Humana went out of business. Either way, many people would suffer. I therefore have to conclude Humana made the correct decision.

I am not at all pleased with the conclusion I have reached. My head agrees with Machiavelli. My heart, however, does not.

Machiavelli builds his method on three approaches: reading, observing, and cogitating. He has diligently read history and read about the deeds of great men in the past. He combines what he has learned through his reading with what he has actually observed in his experience. He is an acute observer and has learned a great deal from his own experience. He then takes what he has read and observed and "cogitates." He thinks and reasons about what he has read and observed and determines what works in practice.

Machiavelli's three-phased approach is amazingly similar to my approach in the class. We draw lessons from what we read about the past, and we draw on our personal experience. We think about the issues and discuss them (cogitate)— all with the aim to learn more about what works, what is effective.

I had not read *The Prince* before I started teaching the class, and so I cannot be accused of copying Machiavelli's method. I didn't even know what it was. I stumbled on it on my own, and I find it ironic that I am Machiavellian in my teaching.

Machiavelli describes the problems modern business leaders face about as accurately as anyone I have read: "It should be borne in mind that there is nothing more difficult to handle, more doubtful of success, and more dangerous to carry through than initiating change... because men are generally incredulous, never really trusting new things unless they have tested them by experience."

Machiavelli gives us a great deal to think about. I am greatly bothered by his view of human nature, but I have to admit that many of his observations are relevant today.

I visited Machiavelli's tomb in Santa Croce when I was in Florence a couple of years ago. His epitaph reads, "*Tanto Nomini Nullum Par Elogium Nicolaus Machiavelli*" which freely translated says, "There is no epitaph equal to such a great name." That great name, I'm afraid, is still a force in today's political world. You can't ignore it.

26.

Management and Machiavelli

Management and Machiavelli has been one of my favorite books for a long time. It was written by Antony Jay and first published in 1967. Jay graduated from Cambridge with first class honors in Classics, became an executive producer with the BBC, and then formed his own management consulting firm.

Jay uses Machiavelli's method "to analyze current and relevant management problems in the light of experience, observation, and history." He draws heavily from literature and history, and I love his references and analogies. The book provides a way of introducing my students to liberal arts, but with a pragmatic, relevant approach. Jay says, "By a judicious use of the Machiavelli method we can learn to recognize which situations and problems are common to large organizations, and see the different results that tend to be brought about by different courses of action.... There are far more lessons, for those who care to read them, in the long annals of history than the few published management case studies."

Management and Machiavelli is over 200 pages, which is a long book for this class. It is not easy reading for the students because Jay is British (his English is a foreign language!), he uses some unfamiliar words and expressions, and he makes numerous historical and literary references that most of the students know nothing about.

For years I have had the students make oral presentations on *Management and Machiavelli*. In my earlier classes this presentation was the only one I taped. I assigned each student a chapter of the book, and the student would make a five-minute presentation on that chapter to the class. Some students did a great job, but most brought little creativity to the project and merely reiterated what Jay said. The presentations were dull, and neither the presenter nor the listeners got much satisfaction from them.

And so I changed my approach. I now still assign the chapter, but I ask the student to "teach" it to the class. Instead of merely repeating all the points Jay makes in the chapter, students are challenged to make it come to life, explaining what Jay means by illustrating with their own examples drawn from their own experience—in short, with their own stories.

This change has made a significant difference. Not only are the presentations more fun for the students to make, they are more fun for the others to listen to. Furthermore, students are able to practice the techniques they have learned in earlier presentations—tell stories, paint word pictures, give personal illustrations. Some of the students become creative, indeed, and many of them have given me new insights and new ways of looking at old problems.

Some of my favorite chapters in the book are based on literary references. I studied *Paradise Lost* in college. While I appreciated Milton's poetic diction, it never would have occurred to me that the poem had any relevance to today's business world. Jay saw the connection:

> Nothing, you would think, could be further from the
> twentieth-century corporation than Milton's epic account
> of the fallen angels taking counsel about their expulsion
> from heaven: a Biblical story recounted by a seventeenth-
> century poet. And yet as you listen to Satan and his crew
> discussing what action they can take, you realize that in
> every important respect the situation is that of a corpora-
> tion trying to formulate a new policy after taking a terrific
> beating from its chief competitor and being driven out of
> the market it had previously depended on. The language is
> high poetry, but the arguments are, *mutatis mutandis*,
> exactly the arguments which would (or should) be
> considered in the boardroom of any corporation in a
> similar situation.

He then proceeds to cite the speeches of Moloch, Belial, Mammon, and Beelzebub. What I find so amazing is that these speeches have even more relevance today. Jay was referring to a boardroom discussion of strategy after a company has lost a market. But today, this is exactly the kind of discussion and argument that would take place in a company that had become the victim of a hostile takeover. Perhaps embattled CEOs should read Book II of *Paradise Lost*.

Jay has a chapter called "The Fearful Symmetry." He discusses the disadvantages of a hierarchy in an organization and recommends a cell structure where people communicate and move much more openly and freely. When I ask about the phrase "fearful symmetry," none of my students knows where it came from. I give students who are doing the presentation on this chapter some help in advance and suggest they read "The Tiger" by William Blake. I get great enjoyment in hearing an engineer, for instance, read to the class...

> Tiger! Tiger! burning bright
> In the forests of the night,

> What immortal hand or eye
> Could frame thy fearful symmetry?

...and then explain that the symmetry of a hierarchy is every bit as fearful as the awesome symmetry of the tiger.

In the chapter, "Chamber of Horrors," Jay cites examples of poor leaders with paragraphs on King Lear, Richard Coeur de Lion, Nicholas II, George III, and Edward the Confessor. This is a challenging chapter for students to present or teach. It's easy to present the traits these leaders personify, it's harder to come up with appropriate present-day examples.

"Gresham's Law of Management" offers a real opportunity for the presenters. They can do a little research and explain to the class what Gresham's Law is (bad money drives out good), and how Jay applies it to management. He says that bad promotions drive out good employees. When a nonperformer is promoted, good performers become disgusted with management and they leave the organization. A lot of the students have experienced this phenomenon, and they can make this chapter come alive through the examples they have experienced.

Most of the students who work in large corporations have experienced the swings from centralized to decentralized management control. In "Centralization or Decentralization?" they get a historical perspective that causes them to think more critically—and creatively—about the issues involved. Jay talks about colonization and how states have traditionally established colonies over the centuries from Athens to Venice to England. He explains how the Roman Empire survived for so long and describes how the Jesuits have maintained control over their widespread priests for so many years. Jay then shows how the same principles are used in the large, multinational corporations of today.

Jay has lots to say about creativity. He has chapters on the creative manager, creative marketing, and creative groups.

The students particularly respond to a related chapter, "Educating for Creativeness." In this chapter Jay is referring to the British educational system in the 1960s. The students are amazed at how relevant his observations are to the American system today:

> And added to this was the terrible attitude of mind which the examination system fosters; the attitude of waiting to be told what to do next, to be given a precise syllabus, a curriculum, and examination date, and someone to make sure they follow the first along the second until they reach the third. For ten years they are conditioned to a steeple-chase way of life: a series of fences labeled first grade, second grade through to eighth or ninth grade, high school exams, college entrance boards, degrees, with a jockey riding them all the time. It is hardly surprising if they emerge with no ideas of their own about what they want to do, but simply waiting for another jockey to ride them at another fence. When it dawns on them that there are no jockeys, and it is their job to build the sort of fence they want, they look baffled and faintly cheated.
>
> An examination, after all, is not a phenomenon which is much in evidence once the days of education are over.

Jay identifies the current national debate on educational reform in this country:

> Few educationalists are enamored of the system, but hardly anyone is prepared to change it. It is the classic case of altering the demand to fit the supply, of refusing to change the product and trying to change the market instead. And since there is no competition, the system is perpetuated.

Throughout *Management and Machiavelli* Jay refers

to Otto von Bismarck. He has more references to Bismarck than to any other individual. I did not know much about Bismarck before I started teaching. I knew that he was the Iron Chancellor and that he had unified Germany in the 19th century, but that was about it. Jay's many references prompted me to do some research and eventually to read two biographies of Bismarck. No wonder Jay refers to him so often. Bismarck was a disciple of Machiavelli. For him politics was the "cult of the possible." Bismarck was unattractive—really awful—in his personal life. But his goal was to unify the German states, and he did. He was one of the greatest diplomatic negotiators of all time. He knew how to use power effectively for his advantage. He did not hesitate to break his word when it advanced his cause. The ends justified the means.

Most of my students are unfamiliar with Bismarck. Some of them have never even heard of him. Instead of a chapter, I assign one student to teach the class about Bismarck and to show why Jay refers to him so often. In several of my classes we have had exchange students from Germany. These have all been superb students, and I have enjoyed assigning them "Bismarck." To my surprise, I discovered that the German students did not know much about Bismarck either. However, when they got into the subject they were fascinated and excited about telling their fellow students about some German history. The hardest thing for them has been covering the subject in just five minutes!

Jay is a genius in applying Machiavelli's methods to business situations. He beautifully demonstrates my point: history is relevant.

27.

Creativity

I started using *A Whack On The Side of the Head,* by Roger von Oech, in 1985. It was first published in 1983 and had a few rough edges, which I liked. Unfortunately, I think, a new edition came out in 1990. I don't like it as much, but it is now the only one available. It has been sanitized and is more politically correct, but it's not as much fun.

I have found this often the case with revisions. Tom Peters's *A Passion for Excellence* is much more carefully written and edited than *In Search of Excellence*, which is a sloppily written book. But it does not have the force, power, and immediacy of *In Search of Excellence*. It was longer and did not sell nearly as many copies. I feel the same way about the sequels to Stephen Covey's *The 7 Habits of Highly Effective People*. They are more smoothly crafted, but they don't have the impact of the first book. Maybe publishers are trying to cash in on a good thing. Whatever it is, there is little risk that this book will come out in a subsequent revised edition.

The first edition of *Whack* contained several features that have been eliminated. I loved the page of problems in the form of equations to be solved by substituting the proper words for letters. For instance, Y. – S. – S. – A. = W., or N. + V. + P. + A. + A. + C. + P. + I. = P. of S. (Solution given later. Keep trying!) I also loved the list of colorful concepts included in the first edition, such as red tape, green thumb, blue laws, golden rule, to which I could readily add green mail, pink slip, and brown nose.

The first edition had a mind-boggling recommended reading list, which is now not included, and it has a rather vulgar drawing, which appealed to me but which apparently did not pass muster with the politically correct censors. It's only a minor difference, but the second edition's "Premature evaluation can prevent conception" just does not Whack me as much as the first edition's more graphic "The danger of premature evaluation is that nothing will be conceived."

In spite of these peccadilloes, I still love the book, and both the students and executives I work with thoroughly enjoy it. Roger von Oech made a great hit when he addressed our annual Business School luncheon in Louisville in 1994. He is funny and he is creative.

Whack is fun to read. Von Oech whacks you into thinking about things differently. Here are some whacks for me:

- Some great questions: "What are three things you feel totally neutral about?" and "What parts of your problem do you associate with tax returns and what parts with poetry?"
- Making the strange familiar: using metaphors. "The key to metaphorical thinking is similarity." We understand something new through its similarity to something

we are familiar with — iron horses, horseless carriages, and my own addition, the information superhighway.

• The "water model of finance": cash flow, float a loan, frozen assets, flood the market, laundered money.

• *Software Manager*: I like your program except for the ending.

Programmer: What's wrong with the ending?
Software Manager: It should be closer to the beginning.

• Pablo Picasso: "Every act of creation is first an act of destruction."

• Question: What do John the Baptist and Winnie the Pooh have in common? Answer: They both have the same middle name.

• Yoda the Jedi Warrior: "Try? There is no try. There is only do or not do."

When I first started using *Whack* in the class, I gave the students a treat and did not require a memo that week. Their memo was optional. Students who were worried about their grades would have the chance to improve their standing with an easy-to-write memo. I thought the book was light reading and did not lend itself to the serious approach of a memo. I was wrong. I discovered the students learned more and our discussions were more productive when they all wrote memos. I made it simple and gave them lots of leeway to be creative: "What whacked you in *Whack*? Why?"

Over the years, some students showed some real creativity. One student printed her memo on a paper towel. It took quite some doing to run the towel through her printer, but she did it—and she got an A+. Another student printed his memo backwards. Being creative, I took the memo into the men's room and held it up to the mirror so that I could read it. I was quite pleased with myself for figuring out how to do this. Later the writer pointed out that I could have turned the paper over, held it up to the window in my office, and let the paper over, held it up to the window in my office, and let the light shine through it. It was simple—he showed me, and I could read it easily. So much for my creativity.

Reading *A Whack* obviously stimulates a lot of students' thinking. They are reminded of what Antony Jay said about education stifling our creativity. Many of them realize that they used to be creative, but no longer. *Whack* is a wakeup call. In 1994 a student suggested that I would foster more creativity if I let students submit something they created in place of the memo—if they wanted to. I liked the idea, and the results have been exciting.

I have received several poems. A particularly beautiful one was written in Thai and then translated into English (I have had five Thai students). This student read her poem in English and we got the feel of the tonal nature of Thai poetry. Students have done drawings, paintings, sculptures, and have been especially creative in the culinary arts. One student created a Kentucky Derby wreath (it was late in April, and in Louisville everybody gets ready for the first Saturday in May). And I have received some extraordinary computer graphics. One, by another Thai student, was a masterpiece. I passed it around to the whole class. None of us could figure out how he created it, let alone how he printed it.

A great number of my students are technicians by training. They are accountants, engineers, computer specialists, or financial analysts. They don't think they are creative. They think that creativity is an exclusive province of artists and advertising types. What they must learn is that everyone is creative—just in different ways. By doing something creative —something different—they can get out of the box.

I am convinced that traditional schooling has stifled students' innate creativity. The insistence on one right answer (the dreadful multiple-choice test) and the application of rational, logical thinking to the analysis of every problem and situation kill curiosity and experimentation. To get through

Creativity and innovation, however, require doing something different, breaking the rules. Creativity and innovation are also fostered by a sense of fun, of play. We don't have much of that in MBA classes or in the workplace. We need to create a climate where risk-taking is encouraged. I deliberately create this kind of atmosphere when the students do the plays later in the semester.

The only way do develop creativity is to start being more creative. Don't just talk about it—do it!

(Give up? Year – Spring – Summer – Autumn = Winter. Noun + Verb + Pronoun + Adjective + Adverb + Conjunction + Preposition + Interjection = Parts of Speech.)

28.

The Tao

*We no more "have" ideas than ideas "have" us;... the creative
process might be simplified if we stopped searching for ideas
and simply made room for them to visit.*
                                                —Robert Grudin

I received a copy of Bennett Goodspeed's *The Tao Jones Averages* for Christmas in 1984. I immediately fell in love with the book. Goodspeed introduced me to new subjects, new books, and new ideas. I had heard of the Chinese philosophy, Taoism, but knew nothing about it. Goodspeed opened up a new world for me, and for the next several years I had fun exploring it.

The Tao Jones Averages is subtitled "A Guide to Whole-Brained Investing," and its thesis is that most Wall Street security analysts are completely left-brain dominant and are not successful investors. You will do much better if you use a whole-brained approach to investing and a good way of learning how to have a whole-brained approach is through the ancient Chinese philosophy of Taoism (pronounced Dowism—hence Tao Jones Averages). The book has considerably more merit than just as a guide to investing. It is a guide to whole-brained management and leadership—a whole-brained approach to living.

As Goodspeed delved further into Taoism he became "fascinated by the strong resemblance between what Lao Tsu, Taoism's founder, advocated—and the characteristics of the right side of the brain that have been discovered by modern science only recently—some 2,500 years after Lao Tsu's death."

The basic writing of Taoism is the *Tao Te Ching*, a book of 82 short chapters or verses, presumably written by Lao Tsu, and which has many, widely varied English translations (it is reputedly the most heavily translated book in English after the Bible). I have enjoyed reading different translations and comparing them. Goodspeed uses Archie Bahm's translation. My favorite is a newer translation (1988) by Stephen Mitchell.

At the start of each chapter Goodspeed juxtaposes a quote from Lao Tsu (or some other Taoist source) with a quote from eclectic sources. A good Taoist goes with the flow, and that is what Goodspeed does. He observes:

> Unfortunately, Western mentality with its analytic ways tends to resist change by making fixity out of flux, or as Lao Tsu would say, it tries to understand running water by catching it in a bucket.
>
> Since one cannot analyze change until after it has happened, our Western approach leaves us dealing with events after the fact rather than as part of the flow. Moreover, our societal disease of what I call "analexia" (our conviction that if something cannot be analyzed or measured, it is not real) is accompanied by our passion for

numbers.... Taoism has the potential of being a catalyst
for freeing the 'fixity' of the Western view.

Goodspeed gives a lucid explanation of how our brains work. The left hemisphere is analytically oriented. It reasons logically and sequentially. It is programmable like a computer, and most of our educational emphasis is placed on developing this part of our brains.

The right-brain hemisphere operates nonsequentially—all at once—and is intuitive and controls feelings and visual perceptions. "Since it is nonverbal, it communicates to us through dreams and 'gut reactions.'"

After reading this explanation, graduate students in business readily see what has happened to them. Because of the emphasis in classes at school and the emphasis of many of their employers, their right brains have atrophied. They work hard at developing their left-brain skills—and, of course, businesses need those skills. But businesses are increasingly calling for more creativity and innovation from their employees—results that originate in the right hemisphere of the brain. We aren't going to be more creative and innovative until we change our emphasis. We must encourage students and employees to develop their right brains.

Largely as a result of what I learned from *The Tao Jones Averages*, I have increasingly changed the emphasis of the class to a more deliberate focus on developing the right brain. I still stress a left-brain activity, writing, but I don't stress it as much as I used to. I now emphasize more right-brain development such as creativity, listening, visual observation, questioning, and intuition. The ideal is using your whole brain. You will be more effective in most situations if you can appropriately use both the left and right sides of your brain. I emphasize the development of the right simply as a remedial process. Students have to make up for all those years their right brains have been in hibernation.

According to Goodspeed, Lao Tsu feels that "left-hemisphere logic is incapable of leading us to the higher wisdom of intuitive knowing....True education comes from unlearning the artificial rules of man....Teaching should not be done by describing and pointing out differences, but by example."

Goodspeed includes Graham Wallas's model of creativity, which has four stages: preparation, incubation, illumination, and verification.

> Preparation is "doing your homework," researching the situation, searching for information, and it is best performed primarily by left-hemispheric skills. Incubation is "sleeping on it," taking a walk, or just reflecting. It takes place when the left brain idles (emits alpha waves) and the right mulls things over in its own nonverbal way. Illumination takes place when the two brains come together, when the left side is able to verbalize the intuitive understanding of the right. This coming together of the two minds can be so powerful that it often produces the enlightenment, the oceanic feeling, that sent Archimedes jumping out of the tub shouting "Eureka." Verification is the process whereby the left brain confirms the validity of the discovery.

Goodspeed says, "the stages of preparation, incubation, illumination, and verification can be classified hemispherically as left, right, both, and left. This suggests, indeed, that creativity and its counterpart, discovery, are whole brained."

About four years ago I came across an even more helpful model of creativity in *The Creative Manager* by Peter Russell and Roger Evans. Both authors are British, and I think they provide some valuable insights into the creative process. Their model is similar to Wallas's, but has five stages: preparation, frustration, incubation, insight, and working out. They describe these stages:

- **Preparation** involves analyzing the task, gathering data, looking for patterns, trying out ideas, and **questioning as-** sumptions,
- **Frustration** occurs when we are unable to resolve the is- sue; feel bored, irritated, or despondent; and doubt our own ability.
- **Incubation** occurs when we give up trying, put the issue on hold, and hand it over to the unconscious mind.
- **Insight** is the inspiration, the "aha," the moment we nor- mally associate with creativity.
- **Working out** involves testing our insights and giving them form.

They further explain how the brain functions during these stages:

If we look at creativity as a process, we see that both sides of the brain play very important roles. Preparation, focusing as it does on analysis, data gathering, logical thinking, and understanding, uses the functions associated with the left side of the brain. During incubation, when no conscious processing of the issue is taking place, it is difficult to say which side of the brain is dominant; both sides are probably equally involved. Insight is primarily associated with right-brain functions, and the working-out phase returns us to the logical, analytical, verbal modes of thought associated with the left side of the brain....

Although some modern approaches to education pay more attention to right-brain skills, many of today's managers were schooled in the traditional way, and thus they are more fluent and confident in left-brains skills than in those associated with the right side of the brain. This educational bias is another reason why many of us tend to focus on the type of thinking we know best—preparation and working out—and leave the insight to occur in its own "mysterious" ways. To be more deeply creative, we need to balance our left-brain skills with those of our right.

Bennett Goodspeed makes a great case for whole-brained management. He makes fun of "articulate incompetents" who are paralyzed with "analexia," our society's compulsion to accept only what can be measured. Like a good Taoist, we should carefully observe the world around us, get in tune with it, and go with the flow. You can't get anywhere swimming against the current.

The Tao of Pooh

Fame or integrity: which is more important?
Money or happiness: which is more valuable?
Success or failure: which is more destructive?

If you look to others for fulfillment,
you will never truly be fulfilled.
If your happiness depends on money,
you will never be happy with yourself.

Be content with what you have;
rejoice in the way things are.
When you realize there is nothing lacking,
the whole world belongs to you.

—*Tao Te Ching*

Goodspeed was inspired by *The Tao of Pooh*, Benjamin Hoff's marvelous little book that "explains Taoism through an examination of A. A. Milne's familiar characters." *The Tao of Pooh* is one of my all-time favorite books. I gave copies of it to the students in my second graduate class and have been using it in many of my classes ever since. I also recommend it to business executives who want to read something that will help them get better control of their time. If they can't learn from this book, then I can't help them.

For many years *The Tao of Pooh* was one of the books I had the students do a team presentation on. It was part of the team projects that the students do toward the end of the semester. The students always had great fun with the book and enjoyed becoming acquainted—or reacquainted—with the Pooh characters. Currently *The Tao Jones Averages* is out of print, and so I am no longer using it in class. I am using *The Tao of Pooh* in its place.

The Tao of Pooh is a *tour de force*. It is written in the style of Milne's *Winnie-the-Pooh*, and even uses the same kinds of illustrations as in the original Pooh books. Hoff wrote a sequel in 1992, *The Te of Piglet*, which I found too preachy and contrived. *The Tao of Pooh* is a Taoist book—it just IS.

Taoism cannot be explained in words. The first two lines of the *Tao Te Ching* say,

> The tao that can be told
> is not the eternal Tao.

This is frustrating for us in the West since we don't think something is real unless we define it. Benjamin Hoff shows us what Taoism is like through the Milne characters, and especially through Pooh who is the quintessential Taoist.

In one of the self-development programs I conducted for my colleagues I had the participants read *The Tao of Pooh*. I was a bit nervous because one of the participants, Nan Ting, is a native of China. Much to my relief and reassurance, she loved the book and was highly enthusiastic about it. She told me she had read a lot about Taoism in Chinese, but this little book explained Taoist philosophy more clearly than anything she had read in her native language. That was a real endorsement and gave me more confidence in using the book in class.

In explaining one of the principles of Taoism Hoff plays

off the sound of *P'u* against Pooh. *P'u* is the Uncarved Block and is illustrated by the bear, Winnie the Pooh. "The essence of the principle of the Uncarved Block is that things in their original simplicity contain their own natural power, power that is easily spoiled or lost when that simplicity is changed."

Hoff adds:

> Knowledge and Experience do not necessarily speak the same language.... You might say that there is more to Knowing than just being correct.... One more funny thing about Knowledge, that of the scholar, the scientist, or anyone else; it always wants to blame the mind of the Uncarved Block—what it calls ignorance—for problems that it causes itself, either directly or indirectly, through its own limitations, nearsightedness, or neglect.

People who try to fit square pegs into round holes ignore "the clear reality that Things Are As They Are." When we know and respect our own Inner Nature, we know where we belong. We need to "recognize Inner Nature and work with Things As They Are."

The most characteristic element of Taoism-in-action is *Wu Wei*, which means literally "without doing, causing, or making." Hoff explains:

> The efficiency of *Wu Wei* is like that of water flowing over and around the rocks in its path—not the mechanical, straight-line approach that usually ends up short-circuiting natural laws, but one that evolves from an inner sensitivity to the natural rhythm of things.

He continues: "The surest way to become Tense, Awkward, and Confused is to develop a mind that tries too hard—one that thinks too much."

This concept of *Wu Wei* helped Bob Taylor and me to

refine our thinking on the difference between managers and leaders. Bob came up with a simple, but profound observation: "Managers *make* things happen. Leaders *let* things happen." The more I have thought about it, I have realized that this concept is basic, and it has greatly influenced my thinking on leadership.

The Bisy Backson is one of the great creations in the book. Derived from the misspelled note, "Busy, Back Soon," the Bisy Backson symbolizes the person who is constantly on the move, scurrying around trying to do several things at once, always trying to work harder and faster. This person never has enough time to finish anything, or, for that matter, to enjoy anything. The Bisy Backson is unwilling to change inside and instead constantly struggles "to change everything (the Bulldozer Backson) and everyone (the Bigoted Backson) else *but* himself."

Hoff points out that we have an obsession with saving time.

> Practically speaking, if timesaving devices really saved time, there would be more time available to us now than ever before in history. But, strangely enough, we seem to have less time than even a few years ago....
>
> The main problem with this great obsession for Saving Time is very simple: you can't *save* time. You can only spend it. But you can spend it wisely or foolishly. The Bisy Backson has practically no time at all, because he's too busy wasting it by trying to save it. And by trying to save every bit of it, he ends up wasting the whole thing.

We need more awareness. We should enjoy what we are doing. If we enjoyed the process, we wouldn't worry so much about saving time. Hoff says that we need to believe in the power that is within us, and then use it.

He then talks about *Tz'u*, which can be translated as

"caring" or "compassion" and which is based on the Chinese character for *heart*. "From caring comes courage," and from this courage comes wisdom. Clever knowledge has no heart; it does not care. Wisdom does. The way to be happy is to "begin by being appreciative of who you are and what you've got."

Hoff mentions *T'ai Hsü*, the "Great Nothing." Our minds are stuffed so full that we cannot see or appreciate the basics, and "a mind confused by Knowledge, Cleverness, and Abstract Ideas tends to go chasing off after things that don't matter, or that don't even exist, instead of seeing, appreciating, and making use of what is right in front of it."

Finally, we can stop looking for the Enchanted Place "because the Enchanted Place is right where you are."

What a beautiful concept! It blows my mind to think what this means. All we—any of us—have to do is look around the room. We are in an Enchanted Place. It's right where we are.

29.

Drawing

Ever since we have been reading *The Tao Jones Averages* and *The Tao of Pooh* I have had the students do a drawing exercise in class. The basic purpose of the exercise is to let the students discover what it is like using their right brains.

The exercise is fun, although not all students enjoy it. I think that they all learn something from it, even those who say "I can't draw." Here's how it works.

I put a blank piece of paper at each student's place. They immediately get suspicious. I give them their instructions: "Draw a picture of the organization you would like to work in in the future. You cannot use any letters, words, or numbers (a chorus of complaints from the engineers in the class!). Your picture can be as abstract or realistic as you want. After you finish your drawing, you will get in groups and share it with the group. Any questions?" I then dump onto the middle of the table a bunch of pencils, colored pens, and an assortment of markers in various colors and styles.

At this point some remarkable things happen. I can just about predict the reactions, no matter what the class—whether it be undergraduate students, graduate students, business executives, or business school professors (I've done this exercise with all of these groups). A few people, no doubt right-brain dominant, eagerly reach for the colored markers and enthusiastically begin. It's as if they have been waiting all semester to do something as fun as drawing a picture. A few sit in sullen silence. They don't do anything. They are unhappy campers, presumably left-brain dominant, who may make a remark like "I never could draw," or "I hated drawing in kindergarten." They just stare at the blank piece of paper in front of them.

The rest fall somewhere in the middle. They quietly pick up a pencil, think for a while, and then start drawing. As they get more into it, they reach out for the colored markers and begin to get more enthusiastic.

Meanwhile, the left-brainers just sit and stare. They don't want to do this exercise, and besides, they are not sure what to do. They don't like it when they are not told exactly what to do. They look at the person sitting next to them, deeply involved in the drawing, furiously coloring, perhaps humming a little tune, and they feel even more despondent. But then they finally pick up a pencil and get something on the paper. Pretty soon they've got something going, and some even ask for coloring markers.

As they get into their drawing, the students as a whole become more relaxed and less self-conscious. There is usually some banter, some laughter, and the markers get tossed around. "I need a green," or "Does anyone have a yellow?" and a missile goes flying the length of the table.

After about ten or fifteen minutes, I call for their attention. "All right. Let's form groups of four. I want each of you to show your picture to the other members of the group.

Don't explain it. Let them tell you what they see in it and ask you questions about it. Then tell them what you had in mind."

The group behavior changes. There is great animation, lots of body language and movement, lots of raucous laughter, much smiling. People unconsciously sit on the arms of the chair, stand up, and even sit on the table. It is by far the most uninhibited communication they have had with each other all semester. Those who are not good artists get good-natured ribbing and encouragement, and those who are good get confirmation and admiring comments. At the end of the exercise, the participants are more positive and upbeat—and happier—than they were at the beginning.

I bring them back to the table and ask, "What did you learn from this exercise?" Some wag always responds, "That I can't draw!"

"All right. What else?"

Soon we get into a discussion about how they communicated through their drawings. They had been able to discern quite a bit from each other's picture. In some groups, the patterns were amazingly similar, while in others they were completely different.

I ask if they were aware how they had communicated with each other in their group. They usually had been too engrossed in what they were doing, and had not observed the process. I then tell them what I observed: how they were so animated and uninhibited.

When I first got my camcorder, I taped this exercise. I taped individuals looking sullen and blank at the beginning (the left-brainers), and I taped the groups, capturing the animation, the movement, the laughter. I would then play the tape back so they could see themselves. The problem was that I am a lousy videographer. I jumped around too much; it was out of focus; it was awful. The students were so busy making fun of the tape that they hardly saw what was on it. I was embarrassed, and so I stopped doing it (it also took up too much time). Now the students have to take my word on how they communicate in the exercise.

What the students learn is the power of the right brain. When we shut down the left-brain dominance and give our right brains a chance to work, we can tap into some significant areas that are usually buried. This is our unconscious mind, and it is such a resource for us if we would only use it. To do this, we have to let go of the logic, the rules, the inhibitions of the left brain and allow the feelings, the creativity, and the playfulness of the right brain to flow forth.

Mind Mapping

The drawing exercise clearly demonstrates that we could undoubtedly communicate more effectively by using more of our right-brain capacity. This leads me into a handout that I give to the students, "Mind Mapping." It's a short article by John Grossman, and I point out to the students that I take my sources where I can find them—this one from *USAIR Magazine*, September 1988. That may not be the most scholarly source, but it's a helpful article on a useful communications tool.

Mind mapping was created by Tony Buzan, author of *Use Both Sides of Your Brain*, as a tool for tapping into your unused brain power. A mind map is a nonlinear way of organizing ideas. You draw pictures instead of writing words. If you were preparing a speech, like most executives, you would probably draw up an outline headed by Roman numerals. The article says this is a mistake and quotes Michael Gelb: "Outlining is a prematurely linear way of expressing your thoughts. You're forced to order your ideas before you come up with them, which puts a severe clamp on your ability to generate ideas."

Instead, draw symbolic pictures, frame them and label them with one word, which you should print, and let your mind free-associate key topics, and then draw lines connecting them. This activity is fun and helps loosen you up to fresh, free-flowing ideas. This is a great technique to get our minds going when we are stymied with writer's block.

The article points out that the better you get with this, the fewer words you need. In giving a speech, you don't need a lot of written notes. Your pictures will trigger your memory, and instead of being wooden and rehearsed, your speech will be more spontaneous and alive. It's more fun to give and more fun to listen to.

You can use mind mapping techniques to plan phone calls or interviews, instances where you can come up with ideas and questions ahead of time. Often we think of something vital after the conversation or interview is over. Mind mapping helps you to think of these points beforehand.

On some occasions when you want to take notes, mind mapping is a good technique. A simple picture will help you recall the main point more clearly. Mind mapping can also be used to set agendas for meetings and for keeping notes during meetings.

Mind mapping is not taught in school—at least in schools that I am familiar with. It certainly isn't taught in business school. And that's a shame, because it's an effective tool and it's fun to use. Why is it our education system rejects anything that is fun? Do we think that if it's fun, then it's not educational?

30.

Genogram-Lifeline Project

My son Michael loves the Kentucky Derby. In 1986 when he was in his second year at the Harvard Business School he came to the Derby with a classmate. Whenever I meet a student from one of the top business schools I like to ask, "What is your favorite course at Harvard (or wherever)?"

When I asked Michael's friend, Olga, she did not hesitate. "It's a course called Career Management, taught by a visiting professor. The great thing we have done is the genogram. That has been fascinating for me, and I've really learned a lot about myself."

"What is a genogram?"

"A genogram is a kind of family tree. You go back as far as your grandparents and interview as many members of your family as you can. You try to find out what they did and why they did it. It helps you understand your family and the values that are passed down through each generation."

I was intrigued. I had begun to believe that greater self-knowledge was a key to becoming a more effective leader. The genogram could be a tool for gaining more self-knowledge. Olga sent me a vast, detailed notebook of materials on the genogram that was used in her class. I could not do anything so ambitious as she had done in her class, but I could modify it and have my students research their own family heritage.

Genogram comes from *genos*, origin or race, and *gram*, something written. I think of it as a psychological family tree that helps you discover the patterns and problems that have been handed down from one generation to another. It basically helps you to clarify your values and gain an understanding of how you got those values.

For the genogram project, the students interview as many of their family members as they can, going back to their grandparents' generation. I give them a list of questions they can explore (see Appendix V). They must draw up a chart, in the form of a family tree, showing names, dates of birth, marriages, and deaths. If they can, I encourage them to include other information such as place of birth, educational level, occupation, and religion.

When I first did the project, I did not insist on drawing up the chart. However, I learned that the project became more meaningful to the students when they could see something on paper. It helped them organize the information and it helped them see patterns that often recur in family histories.

The most important aspect of the genogram project is interviewing family members. I strongly urge the students to use an audio tape recorder—especially when interviewing someone elderly. This tape can become a family treasure. Some of my students have really gotten into this project and have videotaped the interviews. I am a bit wary of videotaping them because my experience has been that most older people are intimidated by the camera. They are not as relaxed and natural in front of a camera. With the audio tape, you can just turn it on and set it aside, and the interviewee soon forgets about it.

In the spring of 1988 we were discussing the genogram project after the completion of the exercise. Students were talking about some unexpected things they had learned from doing it. A student then turned to me and said, "Ballard, tell us about your genogram."

The whole class looked at me expectantly. Sheepishly, I replied, "I haven't done it."

The catcalls were deafening. I thought that they were going to throw me out the door. "All right, all right. I'll do it." And I did.

The next week I called on my aunt, Jane Norton, my father's sister, my godmother, my soul mate, and former owner of Orion Broadcasting where I had worked for eighteen years. We had a marvelous interview of two and a half hours, all of which I got on audio tape. Over the years Jane and I had had many intimate conversations. I loved her dearly and thought that I knew her well. I did not expect to learn anything new from the interview, but I was dead wrong. There's something about asking direct questions—and really listening to the answers. I don't think we do that in our usual conversations. At least I don't.

From the interview with Jane, I got some incredible insights into my father which I had never gotten before—even though we had talked about him many times. I got a whole different picture of Jane's father (my grandfather whom I hadn't known well), and began to understand his influence on his children.

I never knew my paternal grandmother. She died when Jane was eighteen and my father nineteen. They did not talk about her much, and when they did it was usually in impersonal terms. I asked Jane about her mother's death and what it had been like for her.

She was pensive and tears formed in her eyes. She told me how much her mother's death had hurt and how hard it had been on her. I don't think anyone had ever asked her how she felt about her mother's death. At that time and in that culture you just did not talk about these kinds of things. You just toughed it out and stoically went on with your life. Jane gave me a glimpse into herself that she had always kept hidden. That moment was worth the whole interview. I felt a special closeness to her, and I felt her extraordinary inner strength that had enabled her to bear so nobly the successive deaths of her husband and only son.

Four months after the interview, Jane died of a massive stroke. Thank God I had the tape. I played it for Jane's daughter, Mary, after the funeral and made a copy for her. It's our family treasure.

Next I interviewed my mother. I knew I wouldn't learn anything from that interview. That is probably why I had never bothered to do it before. I had heard all the stories—time and again. But I had to do it—or my students would run me up the yardarm.

Again I was totally wrong. I found the interview with my mother not only fascinating, but also enlightening. The question that did the trick was, "When you were growing up, who was the biggest influence on you?" I already knew the answer. It had to be her father. She adored him and talked about him all the time.

I was completely surprised when she answered that it was her grandmother, her mother's mother who had lived with them when my mother was a child. Her grandmother had taught her to sew and was a demanding perfectionist. She had strongly influenced my mother, to the extent that my mother never got over it, becoming a victim of her own perfectionism. I suddenly had a whole new insight into my mother and her perfectionism, and I gained a more tolerant understanding of why she lived the way she did.

One of the things I learned from that interview with my mother is the power of the question: who was the greatest influence on you when you were growing up? It is a powerful question, and if you want to get real insight and understanding of a friend or family member, just ask that question. If that person trusts you, he or she will often open up and answer with amazing candor and frankness.

I now share the stories of my own genogram with my students. If an old geezer like me can get so much good from doing the genogram and interviews, then it must be worthwhile for the students.

I try to make the students aware of the opportunity that doing the genogram gives them to gain greater self-knowledge. Here are some observations I share:

> As an adult, the self-concept you have is largely a relic of the concept you had of yourself when you came out of adolescence and entered your early growing up phase. Unless you have consciously reviewed that self-concept and revised it for the better, you may very likely be carrying around in the back of your mind an unnecessarily negative image of yourself, formed from obsolete data.
> —Ken Albrecht, *The Creative Corporation*

> Each of us has a different reservoir from which we draw. Whatever our heritage, it is our response to and our use of that heritage that make us different. We come into the world with a specific set of attributes, a unique cluster of variables selected from myriad possibilities of people who have preceded us.... If we as adults have not yet discovered this for ourselves, now is a good time to start.
> —Virginia Satir, *The New Peoplemaking*

> Think about how we were programmed and how those programs shaped how we saw the world.... But as we

examine our scripting carefully, many of us will also begin
to see beautiful scripts, positive scripts that have been
passed down to us which we have blindly taken for
granted. Real self-awareness helps us to appreciate those
who have gone before us and nurtured us.... There is
transcendent power in a strong intergenerational family.
An effectively interdependent family of children, parents,
grandparents, aunts, uncles, and cousins, can be a powerful
force in helping people have a sense of who they are and
what they stand for.
—Stephen R. Covey, *The 7 Habits of Highly Effective
People*

The students generally respond to Covey's analogy of
the computer programmer. Most of them think in terms of
programs and programming. But they have not thought about
how they were programmed, who programmed them, and
whose program they are operating under now.

In general, the older students seem to get more out of
the genogram project. Several have turned on and have gotten their whole families involved. Some students have un-
covered an amazing amount of information, while others have
been able to discover little. For some students, the genogram
exercise is painful, and a few have not been able to do it. I
respect the students' wishes. After all, the project is for their
benefit, not mine. A few times in the past I have not been
sensitive enough to what a student was trying to tell me, and I
have regretted it. But for the vast majority of students, the
combination of the genogram and lifeline is a highly rewarding exercise.

The genogram helps students think about their values
in a different way. They realize that their deepest beliefs did
not just come to them out of the blue. They begin to ask themselves, "Why do I believe this?" or "Why is this so important
to me?" When they discover that this belief has been a long-held

value in their family, they get a greater sense of themselves.

The more I have thought about leadership, the more I have determined that self-knowledge is vital. But greater self-knowledge is seldom an objective in the classroom. We seem to constantly pursue the ideal of more knowledge—sometimes at the expense of gaining greater self-knowledge.

The genogram is a useful tool to learn about yourself and your values. With this increased awareness, you can become more confident about who you are, why you think the way you do, and what you want to do in life. This self-knowledge is essential for a potential leader. You must first of all know who you are before you can effectively influence someone else.

Lifeline

The other part of this project is the Lifeline. I discovered this exercise in *The Leadership Challenge* by James Kouzes and Barry Posner, and have been using it for a number of years in conjunction with the genogram. Kouzes and Posner give these instructions:

> • On a blank piece of paper, draw your "lifeline." Start as far back as you can remember and stop at the present time.
> • Draw your lifeline as a graph, with the peaks representing the highs in your life and the valleys representing the lows.
> • Next to each peak, write a word or two identifying the peak experience. Do the same for the valleys.
> • Now go back over each peak. For each peak, make a few notes on why this was a peak experience for you.
> • Analyze your notes. What themes and patterns are revealed by the peaks in your life? What important personal strengths are revealed? What do these themes and patterns tell you about what you are likely to find

personally compelling in the future?

About three years ago I came across the concept of the Group Lifeline in *The Human Element* by Will Schutz. I give a description to the students (see Appendix VI) and suggest they do the exercise on their own. This exercise helps you probe your leadership roles and helps you gain insights into your behavior in relating to others—a valuable insight for understanding more about your capabilities and preferences as a leader.

I don't have the students turn anything in to me. Instead, they meet with me in my office, bringing a copy of their genogram and lifeline which they show me. We first discuss the genogram, and I help them to clarify and understand the values they have absorbed from their families.

They then show me their lifeline, and I ask them what they learned about themselves in doing it. Sometimes I can point out trends and patterns that jump out at me that they were largely unaware of. The way the lifeline is drawn usually indicates if a person gets more satisfaction from achieving goals or from having good personal relationships. Whichever the case, when students understand this about themselves, they can make better career choices. If they are achievement-driven, then they should seek an organization where they will be recognized and rewarded for their achievement. If relationships are more important, then they should seek an organization that has more a sense of "family"—a team that they enjoy being on—and one that will not keep them from devoting time and attention to their own family.

For many students the lifeline is revealing. Sometimes they respond that they are not sure what the lifeline says about themselves. When I tell them what the line—the way they have drawn it—tells me about them, they are surprised and usually say, "Yes, that's me." It's a matter of looking at the line and seeing patterns. For most people, the same kinds of events, achievements, or relationships produce the high points. The object is to discover what these are and to make decisions and live your life so that you will have more of these highs in the future.

The low points are also telling. For most students the lows are caused by some kind of loss—the death of a loved one, an illness (the loss of health), the breakup of a relationship, the loss of a job. Most students see that they have been able to bounce back from these losses. They realize that tragedies are a part of life that we must all deal with.

The reason I don't have the students turn in their genograms and lifelines to me is that they are so personal. The students keep them at all times. I feel that I am treading a fine line between probing and prying. Careful probing can prove helpful, if I maintain the student's complete trust. I tell the students that if there is something they don't want me to know, then don't tell me. I am never judgmental. I am there to help the students discover for themselves. I also do not do any counseling. I am not trained, and my own Hippocratic oath is "First of all, do no harm."

As you would imagine, students make all kinds of discoveries and uncover all kinds of stories. Some run into reluctant parents who don't want to talk about the past. Some students use the class—or me—as an excuse to ask questions they have long been curious about. "Dad, I've got to do this for the class."

Those students who are fortunate enough to have grandparents still living find that the older generation usually loves to talk about the past—and they are usually flattered to have young people interested enough to ask them for their views.

Some students do both their genogram and lifeline on a computer and print out professional-looking documents. Several students have color-coded their genograms, indicating religion, educational level, and occupation each in a different color. One of my students had material and documentation going back to the Mayflower—yes, the Mayflower. The record belongs to a student from India—he could go back on his father's side some fifteen generations. The most creative genogram was done by one of my Thai students. She got photographs of all her family members, scanned them into her computer, and printed a professional-looking family chart with pictures of everyone. No boxes and circles—real people. And what a handsome family!

I've learned several things from my students through this exercise. Siblings see a parent in different ways. It is as if two different people are being described. Family members describe—and see—the same events in vastly different ways. Here's the story of one of my students. Both her grandmothers were still living—and both out of town. She wrote to them, sending a long list of questions about the childhood of their son and daughter (her parents). Each grandmother dutifully responded in great detail. The student then interviewed her mother and father, asking them the same questions. The responses were entirely different from those of their mothers. We always see things from our own point of view.

Some events or themes recur in my students' families more than I had expected. I have been surprised at the number of Baptist-Catholic marriages. In this part of the world, I thought that Baptists and Catholics hated each other—especially fifty years ago. But apparently not. I have also been surprised at the number of divorces—not recently, but fifty and sixty years ago—and the number of divorcees among practicing Catholics. I had thought that there were not many divorces then and that Catholics hardly ever got a divorce.

A theme that recurs in many families, including my own, is alcoholism. I would say that alcoholism in some form appears in the majority of the genograms of my students. In some cases it is severe and deeply affects the entire family for generations. For many years this "problem" was denied and covered up. Now families are more openly confronting it and dealing with it. Many are on the road to recovery, but the scars remain.

Most students are positive about the genogram and lifeline exercise. Several years ago a student wrote this assessment:

> The genogram project was a great exercise. I learned more about myself and my family during that two week period than during the previous 34 years. I have a much greater appreciation of my family's history, our value system, and our beliefs.

Another student wrote:

> This class has allowed me to discover myself and what I want out of life. The most meaningful discovery was made during the genogram and lifeline assignment. I never thought about what makes me happy. I just reacted to my environment. Knowing what makes me happy, I can begin choosing those things in life that will steer me to greater happiness and satisfaction.

Patty's story is poignant. She was from South Dakota. (Incidentally, I have had four students from South Dakota, and they have all been superb. It must be the hard winters.) Patty's husband was a career army NCO and was stationed at Ft. Knox. They had three young sons and had lived all over the place, moving every couple of years. Patty had gotten her undergraduate degree from Kansas State and was getting her MBA at U of L.

Patty was a hard worker, an excellent student, a splendid person with high moral values. But her parents were disappointed in her. She had married her childhood sweetheart right out of high school and had lived the life of a nomad ever since. In South Dakota, according to her parents, you didn't live that way. You put down roots and raised a family in one place, giving them the stability they needed. As a result, Patty felt she had let her parents down. She felt guilty.

As part of the genogram exercise, Patty called her grandmother who lived in South Dakota. Patty had grown up near her grandmother, but she really didn't know that much about her. She said that she could feel the joy in her grandmother's voice as she talked about the past—and what a past it was.

Her grandmother had come to South Dakota from Missouri in a covered wagon in 1907. She had been a real pioneer. Just the previous year (1986) she had flown to Scotland by herself to visit relatives she had never met before. Just think of it. In her lifetime she had gone from covered wagons to jet airplanes. Talk about change!

Patty found a real soul mate in her grandmother. She, too, had her grandmother's pioneering spirit. She no longer needed to feel guilty about it. This pioneering spirit was part of her heritage, and from Kentucky she later moved to Germany with her family where she successfully combined a teaching job with raising a family.

Perhaps the most poignant stories that come out of the genogram exercise are ones where connections are made— most often with a grandmother. Several students have told me how much they appreciated the genogram because it had put them in touch with a grandmother they really didn't know, and it allowed them to establish a bond, a relationship which they cherished.

One day Richard came to my office. He had his two daughters with him. They were about six and four years old. Richard had been in my class several years before, and I had not seen him since.

After a bit of small talk, Richard said, "Do you remember the genogram project?"

"Sure."

"Well, because of the genogram I interviewed my

grandmother. She lived in a small town in southern Indiana. I really didn't know her. I just thought she was some old lady who sat on the front porch in her rocker. It turned out she was quite a character. She eloped at sixteen, had run her own business, and was a real character. After the interview I went to see her often. We formed a strong bond, and I took my girls to see her, too. We loved her.

"She died this past summer. She had become a special person in my life—and I would never had gotten to know her if you hadn't made me do the genogram. I wanted you to know this. I don't know how I could ever thank you."

I was deeply, deeply moved, but managed to say, "You just did." And we hugged.

31.

Plays

All the world's a stage.
—As You Like It

The way the plays came into being in my class is symbolic of the way the class has developed, and is also symbolic of the way I have changed my approach to teaching.

Originally, I used the "group" project to enable students to get more knowledge. I would have a group read a book and then tell the rest of the class what the book said. This was not effective. Neither the givers nor the receivers got much benefit from the effort. I even tried to put grades on the individual and group performances. That didn't last long.

I still felt that some kind of group exercise would be useful, but what? One day I ran into a colleague, Sid Baxendale, and he told me he was using *Antigone* in an accounting class. That started the wheels turning. I had never read *Antigone*, and so I immediately read it. This had real possibilities. That semester I had a group of students present *Antigone* to the rest of the class. The purpose was to illustrate aspects of leadership that the play dramatized. A different group presented *The Tao of Pooh* with the same purpose in mind. Other groups presented more straight-forward books, such as Bennis and Nanus's *Leaders*.

I began to see the advantages of the play. I added *King Lear* and then *Macbeth*. Since the plays came when they did —late in the semester—I began to put more emphasis on creativity. The students were given poetic license to be as creative as they could be. I also realized the project should be "play," that is, fun. Creativity, play, and fun go together. At class reunions, students still talk about being Pooh, or being Cordelia.

When I started assigning *The Tao of Pooh* to the whole class (in 1995), I substituted *Othello* in its place. And so I now assign students to one of four plays: *Antigone, King Lear, Macbeth*, or *Othello*. I give careful thought to the assigning, trying to put students where I think they will do a good job and have the most fun. My casting usually works well. In all the years, I have had only one dysfunctional group—undergraduates—who simply could not work together. I have had a few others that were disappointing, usually because one personality in the group is too dominant, and the group never functions as a team. One *Lear* group was probably my fault. I put four strong personalities in the group. They all wanted to be leaders, and they could never agree on a satisfactory course of action, each wanting to do it his or her own way.

I give the assignments five or six weeks ahead of time and provide copies of the play. I point out that they will need to get together as a group at least a couple of times outside of class. The most difficult thing will be working out the schedule so that they will have enough time to determine as a team how they want to present the play. That means they had better start reading the play and getting organized.

A couple of weeks later I give the students some handouts on each play, articles and essays to give them some ideas to stimulate their thinking on how to approach the play from the perspective of leadership. I also give them an excerpt from Karl Albrecht's *The Creative Corporation* that discusses the danger of groupthink. It stresses the point, "The team should always be better than one individual because of the synergy; the contribution of each individual enhances that of the others." The handout also discusses how the creative team works and that it always starts with a clear sense of purpose.

I want the students to learn and experience what it is like to create a product as a team. I want the final product to be something that no single person could have thought up on his or her own. They must play ideas off each other, ask what-ifs, reverse their thinking—do all the things suggested in *Whack*. They should not go with the first right answer, or let one person in isolation script the whole thing. This is a team project. They all must contribute; this is what synergy is all about. The whole must be greater than the sum of its parts. That's the only reason to work in a team—to produce synergy, to produce something you couldn't by yourself.

I have found that in so many classes we are now emphasizing working in groups. We call it working as a team, but it usually isn't. It is rather several people working individually in a group. That is not a team. The same thing is true in many businesses. We give lip service to teams, but the work is done by individuals doing their own thing and then meeting as a group. Or else the leader takes complete charge and tells everybody else what to do. A team can be effective. But it works only when there is synergy.

Some students ask me, "What do you want us to do?"

I always reply, "I want you to surprise me—pleasantly!" They are so used to following instructions and filling in the blanks. It's time they created something on their own.

I also challenge the students to exercise leadership in

their teams. This means listening to others and bringing out the best in them. It means that they have to develop trust in each other, because they must depend on each other to do what they say they are going to do. I urge them to take risks and to remember that this is a play. It should be dramatic and entertaining.

I love the performances. I can just sit back and enjoy them. It is amazing what students can do when they are given the proper encouragement. When I see genuine enthusiasm from members of a team, I know that it is going to be a good performance. That's part of the secret. If you are excited about it, if you are looking forward to doing it, you usually will do it well.

Each team makes a presentation of about twenty minutes. They then serve as a kind of panel, and we ask questions about the play, their interpretation, and how they decided to do what they did.

Antigone is our longest running play. It lends itself to modern interpretations and adaptations. The students have created some remarkable gender reversals where Creon has been a woman. Antigone has always remained a woman, however. Most of the *Antigone* performances have been adapted to a wide range of modern business organizations, from cigarette manufacturers, to construction companies, to hospitals. Several teams have stayed close to the original, and this has also been effective. One team performed in togas, and Teiresias had a white cane and dark glasses. No concern about anachronisms here!

The themes of man's laws versus God's laws, the individual versus the state, freedom versus order, order versus anarchy, old versus young, and male versus female are so well dramatized in the play. These are issues leaders are still struggling with today, 2,000 years later, and the students are good at dramatizing these issues.

King Lear has so much in it that students have to be

careful not to get sidetracked in subplots. To me, *Lear* brings into focus the primary issue owners of every private business face: succession. How do you choose your successor? Lear did it badly! The lessons of *Lear* can apply to publicly held corporations as well. CBS, Chrysler, IT&T, and W. R. Grace have all had problems with choosing successors, although they have not been as dramatic as those in *King Lear*.

Most of the students' presentations of *Lear* involve the boardroom of a privately held company. The old man—or woman: the students are good at reversing roles—wants to retire. The bad VPs—or children—plot to take over control. The person who should be the next successor is forced out and eventually the company goes down the tubes, and the old man and the plotters lose everything.

In Louisville, the *Lear* analogy hits close to home. About ten years ago the squabble among the Bingham family members received national publicity. The Binghams owned the media empire in Louisville, the daily newspapers and television and radio stations. The three children could not agree on ownership and control, and so Mr. Bingham, who had retired but was still Chairman of the Board, decided to sell the whole thing. The analogies to *King Lear* were remarkable, and were brought out by the more enterprising journalists at the time. In conjunction with putting on their performance of *King Lear*, several students have researched the Bingham story. The parallels to the play are eerie, including Mrs. Bingham's direct quote from Lear himself: "How sharper than a serpent's tooth it is / To have a thankless child."

King Lear has lots to say about other aspects of leadership: the importance of vision, seeing clearly, loyalty, relationships, and love. One team named the company it portrayed "The Lear Optical Company." I naively asked them why they had come up with an optical company. "Because the play has so much about seeing and blindness in it."

"Oh, I see!"

One *Lear* team was especially creative. They went to the producer of Shakespeare in the Park and borrowed costumes. One came elegantly dressed as Lear in all his finery at the beginning of the play. Another was dressed as the Fool and recited clever poetry which she had written. But the one we all remember is Cordelia—in a beautiful, brocaded, floor-length gown. But what made Cordelia stand out was her beard—Cordelia was Jeff!

We all wondered how the group had gotten Jeff to play Cordelia. I think he wondered, too. Jeff was an accountant in one of the larger CPA firms in Louisville. That afternoon he had left the office at five o'clock to come to class. He was crossing the parking lot, carrying the large, conspicuous gown to his car. Just then his two senior partners appeared. He didn't know what to say. They would never believe that he was coming to an MBA class to give a presentation and that he was going to wear the gown he was carrying. Would it be better if they thought he was a transvestite? I never found out what they thought. But at least Jeff didn't get fired. And he was a marvelous Cordelia, beard and all.

Macbeth has had many interpretations. It seems to offer students more creative possibilities than the other plays. One performance that I vividly remember I got to see only on tape. In 1990 I had a blocked artery and had to have angioplasty. I was out for a couple of weeks and could not attend the productions of the plays, but I arranged to have them taped. All the performances were particularly good that year, but *Macbeth* stands out. The students had made a video, and so I technically viewed a video of a video. The play was an elaborate takeoff on Gary Hart's failed political campaign. One of the participants, Stan, got his daughter into the act. She represented the witches with fabulous special effects in the form of dry ice in a cauldron. Gary Hart was magnificently played by Mike.

And then enters this beautiful, voluptuous blonde,

Donna Rice. I thought. "My God, they've gone out and hired a professional model." I couldn't believe it. She was a perfect Donna Rice. Then it all of a sudden dawned on me— "That's no model. That's Sara!" Sara was one of the quietest, most reserved people in the class. But when she put on that blonde wig, she was transformed. She was a natural. It was a marvelous performance by everyone, and we could easily understand why Gary Hart did not get the presidential nomination.

Later I asked the group how they had decided to do a video. They were at first going to tape just the witches' scene. But then one thing led to another, and they decided to tape the whole thing. "It must have taken you a long time to do it," I remarked.

"We probably spent about 14 hours on it. But it was worth it. We really had fun doing it!" An amazing testimonial for graduate students who presumably never have enough time—and to think that some people say "all they care about is grades."

An undergraduate performance of *Macbeth* also stands out. This was a group that I was worried about. I didn't think it had any leadership in it. I challenged each member to assume some leadership and help bring the others out. Did they ever! They did *Macbeth* in rap. They appeared as a rock group, complete with guitar, amps, microphones, and speakers. They wore dark glasses and appropriate costumes. The lead singer was an older student who had been extremely shy in class, hardly ever opening her mouth. She had written most of the lyrics and they were priceless—and she could belt them out. I can still hear the refrain, "Greedy! Greedy!"

Another group took a totally different approach to *Macbeth*. This group was part of the "Pilot" MBA program. The whole class remained together for two years, and so they knew each other quite well. The *Macbeth* team somberly announced that *Macbeth* dealt with the darker side, the hidden side, of our natures. If we do not properly deal with that dark side, we could get into trouble, like *Macbeth.*

Then each of the participants got up and confessed to some seriously dishonest things that he or she had done—in school or at work. It was incredible. I could not believe that I could have selected four people who had all made such serious transgressions. But they had. They were so believable, one nearly crying, and another momentarily losing his voice. The rest of us were dumbfounded. At the end we sat in stunned silence, not knowing what to ask. And then the revelation: it was all a hoax. They had completely taken us in, and I fell for it the hardest.

This performance led us into a vigorous discussion of *Macbeth,* the significance of the witches, and how the team had come up with their approach.

Othello is the most recent addition to the plays. I have used it for a couple of years and got exceptional insights from the first two classes that put it on. The first group presented "OJELLO," a takeoff on the highly publicized trial of O. J. Simpson that was dominating the news at that time. It was amazing how the students adapted the play. Instead of the missing handkerchief, it was the lost sunglasses that played a key part. O. J. was played by an African-American man and his friend, Al Cowlings, was played by a man from Chattanooga, Tennessee. These two started jiving with each other, and it brought down the house. It was a performance that they could never duplicate. It was spontaneous combustion.

The other class took a more intellectual approach to the play. But this group had one huge advantage. In their group was a Moor! Not often in this country can we find a Moor to play Othello, the Moor. Zak was from Tunisia, had a Ph.D. in chemical engineering, and was teaching courses in the Speed Engineering School. He was getting an MBA degree on the side. Another member of the group, Fengjiao, had been born and raised in mainland China. She had been in the

U. S. for about five years, was getting her Ph.D. in education, and had married an American.

These two had fascinating perspectives on *Othello*. When I asked about the obvious racial overtones of *Othello*, Zak responded that he thought the themes were cultural, and not racial. In some societies, he told us, if a husband suspected that his wife had cheated on him, he was expected to kill her.

Fengjiao told us that one of the problems Othello had was a problem of trust. Othello was in a mixed marriage. Fengjiao explained to us that she was in a mixed marriage, too, and for it to work well, you must have the trust of the family as well as that of the spouse. She pointed out that Brabantio, Othello's father-in-law, never approved of the marriage and never trusted him after the marriage of his daughter.

How many people get to cast a Moor as Othello? How many get the insights we were able to get from such vastly different points of view?

One of my hidden agendas has been to interest my students in great literature—and there is none greater than Shakespeare. After all, I am a frustrated English teacher. At the end of the last semester a student warmed my heart when she told me, "I really loved doing the play. I had never read any Shakespeare before—he's great. One of my team members just read the Cliffs Notes. I told him he should read the original—it was terrific!"

Perhaps the most memorable response to the plays came several years ago from two of my students who were systems analysts at Humana. They were responsible for getting a new computer system up and running in Humana's hospitals (Humana owned hospitals then). They told the class that it had been nothing but frustration for them. Their team had been unable to make a breakthrough; they could not come up with a workable solution.

After they had done the plays, the two got together and

persuaded their team members at Humana to try something different—to play. So one night they came in late, wore funny hats, reversed roles, reversed thinking, played the fool, and had a raucous, good time. They also made a major break-through that allowed them to solve their problem. It was the most productive the team had ever been.

A student asked, "Why did you do this late at night?"

"We couldn't let anybody see us. If our boss had seen us in those silly hats, laughing and acting crazy, he would have had a fit. He would probably have told us to get back to work!"

Hamlet had it right: "The play's the thing."

32.

Love & Profit

such was a poet and shall be and is

—who'll solve the depths of horror to defend
a sunbeam's architecture with his life:
and carve immortal jungles of despair
to hold a mountain's heartbeat in his hand
                                                    —e. e. cummings

For many years I searched for a suitable final book for the class. I tried several, but none quite fit the bill. Then I read *Love & Profit*, by James A. Autry, just after it was published in 1991. Right away I knew this was the book I was looking for. It is my cup of tea.

The subtitle of the book is "The Art of Caring Leadership." Autry intersperses poems that he has written among the numerous short chapters that are based upon his experience as president of the magazine group of Meredith Corporation. His thoughts are derived from his many years of experience as a manager, and that approach appeals to me and fits in with the philosophy of the class.

Autry believes that "Good management is largely a matter of love. Or if you're uncomfortable with that word, call it caring, because proper management involves caring for people, not manipulating them." I believe that caring is a significant part of leadership, but a lot of us are uneasy using such a concept in the business world. *Love & Profit* forces us to think about why we are managers and makes us realize that the kind of relationships we have will ultimately determine our effectiveness as a manager or leader.

Autry says that management is a trust, a trust that is placed upon you by those you manage. You get your power from the people you manage. Clearly Autry's view of power is opposed to Machiavelli's. In the business world today, I prefer Autry's view. I think modern organizations are better served by Autry's approach and values, and I feel that men and women in today's world will more willingly follow a leader who lives by these principles.

Autry is helpful in his discussion of managing conflict. A manager must get results through people, which means that you must accept differences of opinions and approach—in other words, conflict. He offers advice that I have found especially useful in dealing with a conflict. "When the disagreement or conflict reaches a point that seems an impasse, I ask, 'What would you like me to do?'" Often the other person just wanted you to listen and understand his or her viewpoint. They can solve the problem themselves.

A lot of students say they like the book but don't care for the poetry. A few students defend the poems, but they are in the minority. The poems have grown on me; the more I have reread them, the more I have liked them. One of my favorites is "Threads." I usually have a student read it to the class.

THREADS

Sometimes you just connect,
like that,
no big thing maybe
but something beyond the usual business stuff.
It comes and goes quickly
so you have to pay attention,
a change in the eyes
when you ask about the family,
a pain flickering behind the statistics
about a boy and a girl in school,
or about seeing them every other Sunday.
An older guy talks about his bride,
a little affectation after twenty-five years.
A hot-eyed achiever laughs before you want him to.
Someone tells about his wife's job
or why she quit working to stay home.
An old joker needs another laugh on the way
to retirement.
A woman says she spends a lot of her salary
on an au pair
and a good one is hard to find
but worth it because there's nothing more important
than the baby.
Listen.
In every office
you hear the threads
of love and joy and fear and guilt,
the cries for celebration and reassurance,
and somehow you know that connecting those threads
is what you are supposed to do
and business takes care of itself.

After they hear the poem, most students have a more

understanding look on their faces. Perhaps a few of them will take another look at the poems in the book. I am reminded of Peter Robinson's *Snapshots from Hell*, in which he describes his experience at Stanford Business School. He says that students who lacked grounding in mathematics were called poets. I think we could use more poets in business and business schools.

The real lesson we must learn if we are going to be effective managers is that we must care—about what we are doing, about how we are doing it, and about the people we are doing it with. We should take a lesson from effective parenting: *tough love*.

33.

Student Observations

In my final interview with a student, Patsy, at the end of the semester in the fall of 1994, she brought up the book, *Chicken Soup for the Soul*, by Canfield and Hansen. She mentioned a story in the book about a teacher who had had her students write down on a piece of paper the nicest thing they could say about each other. The teacher collected the papers and subsequently gave to each student the comments the others had made.

Apparently this exercise had meant a great deal to the students because they had kept their sheet of comments, some even carrying them in their wallets in later years. Patsy thought I might like to try this exercise in our class.

So I did. Here is how it works. I distribute a sheet of paper with everyone's name listed. I ask the students to write the nicest thing they can about their fellow students They turn the completed sheets in to me the following week, and I take them and cut and paste so that I have a sheet of comments for each student. I then distribute the sheets to each student at the last class session.

The reaction of the students has been extremely positive. Some of them have been pleasantly surprised. Most of the comments and criticism they have received in the past has been negative. They seem to be programmed to expect negative criticism. When they see the positive remarks and the emphasis on their strengths they literally beam. The first time I did this exercise, I asked for the students' reactions. The first response was from a happy student who addressed his fellow students: "I just want to say thank you. This is a real ego boost. I had no idea you thought I was so creative and had such a sense of humor."

In another class, a student remarked that the comments *in toto* emphasized his strengths and captured him quite accurately. "You might as well remain true to yourself," he said, "because you can't fool your fellow students by trying to be something else."

One woman was getting ready to go into the job market. "I wish I could attach this to my résumé," she said.

We got a laugh from one student who seemed to have difficulty accepting compliments. "This is fine," she said, "but when are we going to get the negatives?" The class hooted her down. They were enthusiastic about following Johnny Mercer's admonition, "Accentuate the positive—eliminate the negative!"

The project has proved to be quite a learning experience for the students—and for me. The students learn on both the giving and receiving ends of the exercise. They learn how difficult it is to write something that will be meaningful to the recipient. It can't be generic; it must be specific and personal. For some it is hard to write just a brief phrase or sentence.

On the receiving end, they can quickly appreciate the thoughtful, caring observations that show insight. Again, these are the personal, specific comments that show the writer had carefully observed and had thoughtfully expressed the observation in a manner that would be meaningful to the recipient.

From the comments of several of the international students—students who had difficulty with English—I learned how important a smile is in communicating. A smile represents a universal form of communication; we all respond more warmly to it.

The exercise also confirmed the importance of using care with the written word. If you are putting an opinion in writing, make sure it says what you mean to say. So many terms and phrases are ambiguous. (I should be more careful with my comments on students' papers, too.)

I probably learned even more than the students from this exercise. It made me realize the tremendous power we all have as potential leaders: the power of honest praise. It has to be specific and it has to be genuine. Too often, I have not used this power when I had the opportunity to do so. I have just assumed that someone else has known when I thought he or she had done a good job or good work. Praise and recognition are powerful motivators when used with discretion—overuse is probably just as ineffective as underuse. The point is, though, it is a power that we all have, but it is worthless if we don't use it.

I also learned that there is real skill in giving helpful comments. Those who seem to do the best job have a great sense of empathy. They think about the person they are writing about. They put themselves in that person's shoes and then write with a greater understanding of what will be meaningful and helpful to him or her.

The exercise helped me relearn the importance of self-confidence, of recognition, and of praise in everyone's life. All good leaders seem intuitively to use this knowledge in creating better relationships with their followers. Teachers need to use it too. It is a powerful motivator.

As is so often the case, Shakespeare seems to have realized all this. In *The Winter's Tale* he says:

> One good deed dying toungueless
> Slaughters a thousand waiting upon that.
> Our praises are our wages.

34.

Last Class

The last class is an opportunity for me to get assessments from the students and to get their suggestions for improving the class. They have now experienced the journey, and they are in the best position of anyone to tell me how to make it better for the future.

The memo for the last class is simply, "Your assessment of this class and me (include any suggestions for improvement)." I have one final conference with each student —the exit interview—following the last class. This final meeting allows me to probe more deeply a student's suggestions, allows us to discuss the student's future plans and continued learning, and allows us a more personal good-bye. Just as I think initial greetings are important, I also think a proper farewell is appropriate. I like to thank the students for their contribution.

Assessments

In the class we do several assessments. I have the students give their anonymous ratings of the guests, based on how valuable the guest was to the students' learning. I try to stay away from a popularity contest. I don't make a big deal out of this, but I found out that if I don't ask the students the direct question, I don't know what the situation is from their viewpoint. Occasionally, I am surprised at the students' assessment of a guest. It was harder for me to figure out undergraduates' ratings. I seem to be more in tune with the graduate students.

The most interesting thing about the assessments of the guests is that every guest will be number one on someone's assessment. The students are not like sheep; they have vastly different personal preferences. The important thing about these assessments is that they keep me in tune with the students. The guests come for the benefit of the students, not me.

I have devised a simple way to assess the books we read. I list all the books on a flip chart. I ask the students to write down on a piece of paper the top two or three books in terms of value to them. I then go down the list and ask for a show of hands, "Who wrote down *Elements of Style*?" And on down the list.

I have the students write down their preferences. Otherwise, they will be influenced by their peers. It's hard to raise your hand when you look around the room and see no one else doing so. If you wrote it down, it's easier to raise your hand—and the assessment is more accurate.

I then do the same thing in reverse. What books were of the least value to them?

The fascinating thing about the book assessments is that no two classes are alike. When I teach two sections of the course during a semester, the assessments are entirely different in each section. Each class develops its own personality and preferences. This holds true from semester to semester. I have seen the least favorite book become one of the favorites in the next semester. I have given up trying to figure out why.

The major part of the class assessment is the questionnaire. Two weeks earlier I had given the students a questionnaire that lists most of the activities in the class—from memos to oral presentations to discussions to guests to genograms— sixteen items. The instructions are simple:

> Answer in terms of *value* to you in the development of your learning, career, effectiveness—not necessarily whether you liked it or not, although I'd like your comments on that, too.
>
> To keep it simple, if the issue is basically satisfactory write "ok"; if it needs more emphasis, write "more"; if it needs less emphasis, write "less." Write any additional comments that you think would be helpful to me in trying to make this course better. Write "n/a" if you did not participate. You don't need to sign this.

The students return the completed questionnaire the week before the last class. I carefully record all their responses and comments and read them to the students in the last class. I have been doing this for years, and it has been the single, most useful tool I have found in helping me make improvements in the class. When a number of students say they want "more" of a certain activity or exercise, we discuss it and see how we can do it. One day a student pointed out that I had a Total Quality approach in my class and this was a part of a continual improvement process. I didn't know anything about TQM when I started doing the questionnaire. I just wanted to find out how to make the class better.

The last item on the questionnaire is "One thing that would make the biggest improvement in the class." I read each response to the class. Some of the suggestions get no support from the rest of the students, some have merit but just can't be implemented without major changes to the class, and some get a positive response and I subsequently make them a part of the class.

At this point I give the students "Ballard's Bibliophily." I tell them that their dictionaries will be of no use—I coined the word. It's simply *books I like* (see Appendix III). I update my list each semester, adding new discoveries and dropping one or two off so that the list does not become too long. I go over the list, telling the students something about each book. I try to set the hook. I want them to keep on reading.

Articles

For the last class, I have the students read two articles, both from the *Harvard Business Review*, and both published around the time most of the students were born. The first is the "Myth of the Well-Educated Manager," by J. Sterling Livingston. Livingston points out that much classroom teaching and much management training are not effective in helping would-be mangers learn what they need to know. Twenty-five years ago Livingston said, "What takes place in the classroom often is miseducation that inhibits their [managers'] ability to learn from their experience. Commonly, they learn theories of management that cannot be applied in practice, a limitation many of them discover only through the direct experience of becoming a line executive and meeting personally the problems involved."

He concludes, "But the main reason many highly educated men [and women] do not build successful managerial careers is that they are not able to learn from their own first-hand experience what they need to know to gain the willing cooperation of other people."

He quotes Alfred North Whitehead's wonderful line, "the secondhandedness of the learned world is the secret of its mediocrity," and says that we must teach aspiring managers to learn from their own firsthand experience, not the secondhandedness of the typical classroom.

Most of the students think the article is still relevant today. I include the article to get them to think about their education. Some of them naively come into the MBA program thinking that it will transform them into an accomplished manager. A theme of this class is that they are responsible for their own learning and they had better start learning from experience, as well as the classroom.

The second article is a short little gem called "Whose Fault Was It?" by Charles I. Gragg. Actually the article is an unfinished essay found in Gragg's papers after his death. He had been a professor at the Harvard Business School, and the article was published in the 60s. I am grateful to David Dillon, President of Kroger, for sending it to me.

Gragg starts off with Hamlet's preoccupation with the question, "Whose fault was it?" He discusses the futility of the question and suggests a more useful question is, "What happened?" It clears the way to action. Trying to assess fault creates all kinds of emotional negatives and defenses. It makes the questioner a judge and accuser and often prevents constructive action to repair the situation.

When we seek to blame others for what went wrong, we are really trying to make them feel guilty. Instead, our focus should be on what we need to do now so that it won't happen again.

Gragg concludes:

> Persons living in an atmosphere in which there seems to
> be a necessity to find out whose fault everything is tend
> almost inevitably to lose much of their spontaneity. (By
> spontaneity I mean the ability to respond to a situation
> with one's whole self and full resources.) One learns to
> play things cautiously, to minimize his risks. One's

freedom and ability to experiment and innovate are curtailed—to say nothing of one's capacity to enjoy, for full enjoyment requires full concentration.

All persons in positions of authority over others, whether they are parents in the home or bosses in the office, can choose between holding those under them responsible for their actions, good and bad, or holding them responsible only for what goes wrong. The leader or administrator who decides on the first choice will, I think, find himself better served than he otherwise would be. Further, if he applies this principle to himself as well as to others, he himself will have his own full resources and abilities free for constructive thought and action.

The article holds a mirror up to us the next time our first response is, "It's not my fault," or "It was your fault." We need to get out of the blame game.

Advice

In my early days of teaching I would encounter puzzled, disbelieving looks on the first night when I told the students what we were going to be doing in the class. They were skeptical, and I don't "blame" them. The approach was different from what they had experienced in most of their schooling. It occurred to me that they would more readily accept the advice of their peers. So I have had each member of an outgoing class write one paragraph of advice for the students who will be taking the class next.

I have the students read their paragraphs to the class. Some of them are funny and clever evoking a lot of laughter, and some are more serious and thoughtful evoking remarks of approval. The students turn them in to me, and I make unedited copies that I cut and paste for the next students. Here are samples of advice from recent years:

• Life is an experience. Some experiences challenge you and cause real growth. This is such a class. You will laugh and celebrate as you discover strengths you didn't even know you had. In a caring, supportive environment, you will work on your weaknesses. You will celebrate with others as they discover themselves. Don't be afraid to discover who you are. You have talents and strengths no one else has...Open your heart, mind, and spirit.You will be glad you did.

• Forget about the old way of learning. Do not expect to be taught anything. You are on your own and you will either learn or not learn. *You are in graduate school for crying out loud*, so think some new thoughts for a change. (Regurgitating in class is frowned upon.) Stir up a little controversy, or test-fly some old notion you haven't shared with anyone. Criticize the assigned reading. Just be prepared to explain yourself. Have fun, be creative, and remember the immortal words of Grace Slick, "Bored is stupid."

• Think of the Leadership class as a quest—a quest for yourself, a quest for knowledge, a quest for life skills. Keep an open, trusting mind and let Ballard guide you to the end that is likely to be a good beginning.

• "Leadership" provides an opportunity to show your creativity in a way that you never have before. This class has few restrictions. If it feels right, do it. Do not be afraid to take chances or do things that are typically out of character. Not only do you learn from Balllard and your peers but you learn more about yourself, your feelings and your career. Ballard and Leadership have taught me more about myself than any person or any thing has to date.

• Welcome to the only business class on earth that draws equally from Machiavelli and the Dalai Lama. Be prepared to share your most guarded feelings about love and profit. Don't take yourself too seriously, or your reading assignments not seriously enough. If you find yourself wearing a finger puppet and speaking in the voice of Tigger, Eeyore, or Pooh, try to suspend your disbelief. Jettison your hard earned cynicism for just one class. Enjoy! We did!

• Don't freak out when you see the reading list! *Fortes fortuna juvat*! There is plenty to read in this course, and you will learn with every reading. When this class is over, you will know more about yourself and your classmates than you would ever have imagined. You will learn, you will grow, but be careful, you will have fun too. This class is the *magnum opus* of business school, and is *mirabile visu*.

• Open your mind. For one brief semseter you will have an opportunity to see the human side of business, apart from the statistics, the financials, the charts and the numbers. Most of the MBA is about the science of business. This class is about the art. It can be a lot of fun to be an artist.

•I always heard this class was great so I signed up for it. The first night when we were hit with reading all these books and making so many presentations I kind of wondered what I had gotten myself into. Don't worry about it. Take it easy, have fun with it, and do what you can. Don't feel you have to read every word of every book and don't struggle over your memos and presentations. It will come to you. Don't be a Rabbit or an Owl or an Eeyore or a Tigger! Be a Pooh!!!

• Get ready! You are about to have a learning experience
you will never forget. Is there a catch you ask? Of course,
the catch is you have to give to receive. Ask questions.
Participate in discussions. Open up in class. Listen
intently. If you don't, the only thing you have to lose is
the most rewarding, challenging, and fun experience of
your education.

• Take a good look at yourself right now because your life
is about to change. Over the next few weeks you will be
given the opportunity to learn about leadership, people,
and most of all—yourself. This class will be time consum-
ing, frustrating, and embarrassing, but you will thank
yourself later. Just keep in mind that this is the toughest
class you will ever love.

• Leave your masks and baggage at the door. You will
learn more about leadership and yourself when you let
down your defenses and open up your mind. Relax and
enjoy. Soak up the wisdom and experiences of your
classmates and teacher. Share your opinions and experiences with the class so they can learn as much from you as
you learn from them.

• This class is like bungee jumping in that the farther you
jump away from the bridge, the more you get out of it.

• If you're not ready to change your life, drop the class.
You'll learn more practical material in this course than
you will have learned in the rest of your courses combined. You will get your maximum semester allowance of
reading, public speaking, and listening—and I don't mean
listening to the professor, but to each other. I hope I don't
shatter your expectations when I say you will learn more
from each other than you will from Ballard. Ballard is a

facilitator of learning, not a drill instructor. So get used to it. And enjoy.

Success

For the last class with both students and executives, I have asked them to write their one-sentence definition of success. Since everybody who is getting an MBA, or who takes the Effective Executive program, is interested in some form of success, I think it is helpful to give some careful thought to what success means to you. We are often caught up in somebody else's definition of success. Once you have a clear idea of what success means to you, then you can make sure you are living your life in such a way as to be successful. I don't think we achieve success. I think it is more of a process. You must know what is important to you, and live your life accordingly.

Several of my students, after having thought about what success was for them, concluded that the way they were living their lives would not get them there. They were not focusing on their real priorities.

I have the students read their definitions to the rest of the class. This is always interesting, and the students enjoy hearing each other's points of view. Some of the definitions are extremely thoughtful. I collect the definitions, telling the students that I am compiling a Success Dictionary.

Several years ago a student asked the class, "How many of you think your definition of success has changed since you have been taking this class?" A number of hands went up.

"How many of you think your definition is the same?" Some more hands went up.

"How many aren't sure?"And a few more hands went up.

Another student looked at me and said, "You could easily find out."

"How?"

"Just have the students write their definitions the first night of class, and you keep them. Then have them write their definitions at the end. You can then compare the two."

I've been doing that ever since. I don't try to prove anything with it, but the students find it fun to compare the two definitions.

The one written on the first night is, of course, right off the top of their heads. Presumably the last one will be more carefully crafted and more thoroughly thought through. The conclusions are predictable. Some of the definitions are word for word the same. Some are similar in theme, but the later one is more thoughtfully expressed. And some are so completely different that you would think two different people wrote them. Statisticians could prove anything they wanted to with these results. I just want the students to have a better sense of who they are and what is important to them. I'm not proving anything.

We have had some memorable definitions of success over the years. Here are some of my favorites:

• A successful person is one who gives all he can to those things that are most important to him.

• Success: To play all the right notes in the right place at the right time.

• Success is having earned the respect of my students, the esteem of my colleagues, and the love of my family.

• Success: Doing what I enjoy and leaving the world a better place for having done it.

• Success is going to sleep at night comfortable in the knowledge that if you do not awaken, someone, somewhere will nod their head and say, "That person had a significant positive impact on my life."

• Success is being healthy, being happy to go to work, being happy to come home, being in harmony with the Lord, having the respect of your fellow workers, and the love of your family.

• Success is getting rich at doing what you love without losing the things that money can't buy.

• Success: To realize my goals by working honestly and caringly and to share the rewards of my labor with the people I love.

• Success is that inescapable inner voice in hearty agreement with our actions, carried out over a lifetime.

• Success is looking back and being able to say that you did what you felt was right and not what you thought was expected.

• Success is living up to your expectations of yourself.

• Success: To know the difference between your needs and wants, and to have all your needs met.

• Success: A state of mind reached when you know, whatever situation you have faced, that you have done your best, treated people with respect, gone the extra mile to achieve what you believe in, taken the time to enjoy yourself, and helped make the people you came in contact with better off for having known you.

• Success: An invitation to the White House in recognition of a personal achievement that has a lasting effect on improving people's lives.

• Success is the achievement of my heart's desire: interesting, worthwhile work to do, balance between my professional and personal lives, and the sense that I've made a difference in the grand scheme of things, whether for a company or a person.

• You are successful when you like yourself and you like what you are doing.

• Success is the state where hard work and passion have come to fruition in attainment of a goal.

• Success is the satisfaction that comes from a life lived with courage, integrity, and service.

•Success is a confidence in your abilities and your choices.

• Success is looking in the mirror and realizing that the person staring back at you is a great person.

• Success is learning to enjoy what you have.

While we are discussing the definitions of success, a student usually asks me, "What is your definition of success?" For a long time I was in somewhat the same position I had been in with the genogram: I didn't have one. I could recite one, but it wasn't really mine. I would use, "Living a life that is important to me," which I picked up from a program at the Center for Creative Leadership in Greensboro.

And then one day it just came to me: "Giving more than I get." Hardly profound, sophisticated, or well-articulated. But it's my definition and it works for me. In any situation, if I approach it with the idea of giving and not getting, I am going to be more successful in dealing with that situation. The same thing holds for a relationship. It's what I can give that matters—not what I can get.

In any circumstance where I am called on to perform, I always try to give more than is expected of me. Serving on a board of directors, for instance, what I concentrate on is what I can give, what I can contribute, not what I can get out of it. To me, the ultimate is making a difference for the good in someone else's life. It's the gift I can make. If I give it, then I will be successful and my life will have been worthwhile.

I got an unexpected reaction to my definition from one of my international students—a Muslim. In our final meeting he told me, "Your definition of success sounded familiar to me. I went home and read the Koran and found it there. I can't translate it precisely, but it was exactly what you said."

His remarks made me think. When I came up with my definition I was only thinking about what works for me. I had no idea I was quoting the Koran. But when I think about it, I have tapped the wisdom of the ages. After all, the Bible says, "It is more blessed to give than to receive."

I end the class with about ten minutes' remarks on leadership. I think it is important for me to share my views in a kind of summary form, and I look at leadership from five aspects: trust, self-knowledge, relationships, caring, and choice. I will cover these views in greater detail in the next chapter.

35.

Leadership

Occasionally I give seminars in leadership. The groups I work with are usually business executives, but I also have worked with executives of not-for-profit organizations, school principals and superintendents, and teachers. Over the years I have refined my thinking on leadership and have distilled what I have learned from my teaching, my experience, and my reading. I claim no originality. Everything I use I have learned from someone else. Many of my thoughts have been shaped by the books we read in class. I have also been strongly influenced by the work of Stephen Covey and have incorporated many of the ideas he so beautifully expresses in *The 7 Habits of Highly Effective People*.

I believe that you can learn to be a leader. It is not something you are born with. Although I recognize that some people are born with more talent than others, I still think that your leadership abilities are not determined at birth.

In the broadest view, I have two premises that affect

my thinking on leadership. The first is that real leadership comes from within. It depends on what you have inside you. You do not become a leader because you are given a title or authority by someone else. Hence the importance of knowing who you are and what you believe in. Until you come to grips with yourself, you cannot lead someone else.

This premise strongly affects what I teach about leadership and the way I teach it. There are no magic formulas for becoming an effective leader. There is no set of traits you can adopt to become a leader. It all depends on what you do with what you are, with what you have inside you.

The second premise is that there are two aspects of leadership that are often in conflict—what I call *spiritual* leadership and *political* leadership. Spiritual leadership is exemplified by such leaders as Gandhi, Martin Luther King, Jr., and the Dalai Lama. These leaders appeal to ethical and spiritual values—the ideals that most of us subscribe to and would like to live up to. Political leadership is exemplified by Machiavelli in *The Prince*. It is the world of action and power. It is driven primarily by our need for security. We expect our national leaders to defend us and protect us from all enemies. They must ensure our survival as a nation. The same is true of a business leader. That leader is expected to take those actions that will assure the survival of the enterprise. Shareholders and employees look to the leader for their security.

Both aspects of leadership are needed. The conflict arises because, in reality, the political leader cannot consistently live up to the high ethical standards of the spiritual leader and still do those things necessary for the security of the nation or organization. Compromises must be made. Often the leader faces choices between two evils. Someone is going to be hurt by the decision, but the decision must be made for the overall good—and survival—of the organization. Machiavelli had it right: the ends sometimes do justify the means. That is reality, and to ignore it would be to deny the horrors of man's inhumanity to man in the twentieth century.

As I have thought about leadership, I have found it helpful to think of it in five aspects. Of course, such an analysis is arbitrary. Leadership works as an organic whole, not through separate parts, but this approach has helped me get a better understanding of what leadership is all about. My five aspects of leadership are:

1. Trust
2. Self-knowledge
3. Relationships
4. Care
5. Choice

Trust

Trust is the *sine qua non* of leadership. Without trust a leader will not be effective over any length of time. People will not willingly follow a person they do not trust.

How do we build trust? We build trust by being trustworthy. This is not just a play on words. What makes a person trustworthy? I think it's two things: character and competence. Character implies integrity, and integrity is basically your behavior over time. You do what you say you will do. People can count on you. Your integrity is expressed in your actions—what you do on a consistent basis and how you treat people.

As Robert Grudin said: "Of all the major ethical nouns in English 'integrity' alone lacks a concomitant adjective, neither 'integral' nor 'integrated' adequately conveying its meaning.... Integrity is psychological and ethical wholeness, sustained in time." You can't have a little integrity or integrity some of the time. You either have it or you don't. It can't be modified.

Competence comes through experience and practice. It means developing the skills to do the job. It means continually learning, working, practicing those skills. It means learning from your experience and your mistakes. To be trustworthy you must have both integrity and competence.

What is apparent to me here is that integrity is in the realm of the spiritual leader and competence is in the realm of the political leader. The ideal is to blend the two.

I think we also create trust by being trusting. We must trust those people we work with. We must take the lead in giving them our trust. We must take the risk and go first, being willing to open up and reveal something of our true selves. Such a move takes courage and a great deal of self-confidence.

The more I have thought about trust and how to create trust, the more I find I focus on respect. When you respect someone you create an atmosphere where the other person feels trusted. When someone respects me, I immediately respond to that person in a more positive manner. I can be more honest and open; I don't have to be defensive. When we feel a leader respects us and our opinions, we actually feel inspired by that person and want to give him or her our best effort.

I think that great leaders respect their followers, just as great teachers respect their students. What better way to show trust in followers than to respect them? Respect comes from within. When you genuinely respect others and their opinions, you create the climate of trust that is a must for leadership.

Self-knowledge

Since leadership comes from within, you must know who you are, what you believe in and why, where you want to go and why, who you want to be and why. Those who do not know themselves cannot effectively influence others.

We must probe deeply within ourselves to discover who we are and what we want to do in life. I have found the genogram and lifeline excellent tools for self-discovery. Both our genes and our environment have affected who we are, the way we think, and the values we believe in. I think it makes sense to explore our past and to try to learn from it. The better we can understand our past, the better we can determine who we are, who we want to be, and where we want to go.

Another helpful exercise is to picture yourself in the future. Some people like to use the deathbed scenario, but I find it a bit morbid. Instead, I suggest imagining that you are old and approaching the final years of your life. Look back and think about your life and what you have done. What are your regrets? Most older people I have talked with regret more what they have not done than what they have done. This exercise can help us make the decision to take a risk and try something, because we realize that we will always regret it if we don't try. This was certainly my experience when I thought about going into teaching—or more precisely, when I thought about not going into teaching.

I have found that asking questions is one of the best ways of probing, and my model is one of the greatest teachers and questioners of all time—Socrates. Socrates' fundamental question was, "What course of life is best?" We usually avoid such a question because it is hard to answer. But a good leader is willing to ask it, and I think we must ask it and try to answer it.

In my searching within myself, I have found it helpful to ask, "What do I need?" and keep asking "Why?" This helps to get at those values that are deeply held and sometimes deeply buried. I don't find it nearly so useful to ask, "What do I want?" The commercial world seems to deal in wants. We need to explore our needs, not wants, if we are to discover our true selves.

In *Money and the Meaning of Life*, Jacob Needleman says that in the *Inferno* Virgil explains to Dante, "Hell is that state in which we are barred from receiving what we truly need because of the value we give to what we merely want." I was so fascinated with this quotation that I read not only the *Inferno* but the entire *Divine Comedy*. I did not find these words in Dante's poetry, but maybe I'm not as an imaginative reader as Mr. Needleman.

As we learn more about ourselves, we can more readily determine what is important to us and what our priorities are. Leaders know their priorities. Without exception, every effective leader I have known has had the ability to focus on the priorities—what is important and will make a difference. They do not get results by fooling around in trivia.

Relationships

When you think about it, leadership is about relationships. Without followers, by definition, there is no leader or leadership. Relationships are key to leadership. How do we build relationships? Primarily through communicating. And that is why communicating is so important for a leader. We connect through our communication. With no connection, there is no relationship. As T. S. Eliot explained it, "Hell is where nothing connects."

Why do we communicate? I think we communicate basically to get a desired response from the other person. Sometimes we don't know what response we want or are trying to get. Often even when we do know the response we want, when we don't get it we keep communicating the same way, only more frantically. We have all seen the boss get frustrated and start shouting and yelling when a subordinate obviously didn't understand the request or demand. This behavior almost always makes matters worse. I have seen the same thing with teachers complaining that their students didn't "get" the lecture. What do they do? They lecture more furiously and rapidly, and the students remain in the dark.

When we don't get the desired response, we must change how we are communicating. We need different skills.

That's why listening is such an important communication skill for a leader. What better ways to "respond" to someone than to listen to that person? Leadership is an influence process, and we have a much better chance of influencing others if we first show our respect for them and genuinely listen to them. They in turn will more likely respond to us.

The amazing thing about listening is that virtually none of us has had any formal training or schooling in how to listen. Early in school we were taught how to read, how to write, and to some extent how to speak. But nothing about listening. We are just supposed to know how to listen. But it's not that simple or easy. It's hard work, and it starts with our attitude. Through listening we show our respect for the other person, and this is the way to build a relationship. Building relationships is an act of creation. We create relationships, and, of course, through relationships we build community.

Leadership always exists in the framework of community. Communications and community come from the same Latin root *communis*, common. Community implies a common set of beliefs and values. We simply won't willingly follow a person who does not share our beliefs and values. Community is built on relationships, and relationships are built on trust and respect for each other.

Care

> *In work, do what you enjoy.*
> *In family life, be completely present.*
> —*Tao Te Ching*

I know that good leaders care. They care about what they are doing, they care about their organization, they care about their people, they care about themselves and their mission. When you care about someone, you set high challenges for that person; you want to see that person develop to his or her full potential. You simply will not settle for second-rate or mediocrity. You give it your best. You have high standards and you do your best to live up to them.

Care, in my mind, is similar to *coeur*, the French word for heart. Care comes from the heart. I don't think you can teach anyone to care. Caring is an attitude of the heart. It develops deeply within a person, and I think it is essential to leadership.

Caring, to me, implies a focus on or attention to the present. You live in the present—now—not regretting the past or worrying about the future. You are present—right now at this moment—in your relationships and your work. You bring enthusiasm to what you are doing—now—and through this enthusiasm you bring energy and joy to your work and to those you work with.

I think this concept of caring includes not only a focus on the present, but also a focus on priorities. Good leaders know their priorities and they intensely focus on them. They have the ability to give their complete attention to whatever is important, and they are tenacious in sticking to the mission—all because they care so much.

The way we care also deeply affects our ethics. I think all our ethics involve a level of caring. Ethical leaders care about others and how their decisions will affect them. Our ethics are always reflected in our actions, and how we treat people reflects how we care about them.

The whole basis of leadership is the act of caring and giving. Leaders give themselves to others. They serve others, and in that serving they find incredible joy. In his *Autobiography*, Gandhi describes his love of nursing (he lovingly nursed his dying father):

> Such service can have no meaning unless one takes
> pleasure in it.... Service which is rendered without joy
> helps neither the servant or the served. But all other

> pleasures and possessions pale into nothingness before
> service which is rendered in the spirit of joy.

Leaders "take pleasure" in serving others, as Gandhi demonstrated in his remarkable life. These thoughts also apply to teachers. Great teachers take pleasure in serving students, and in this serving they find incredible joy.

In this joy leaders also can find a sense of awe, of wonder, and an appreciation of beauty—in nature, in art, and in relationships. I think this sense of awe and wonder is important for a leader. It brings about humility—no leader can get results alone. The appreciation of beauty is important for a leader in that it helps to develop the imagination and the sense of the ideal. Because of a heightened imagination and sense of the ideal, the leader is able to develop and articulate his or her vision more fully. In spite of George Bush, the vision thing is vital to leadership.

Choice

Viktor Frankl survived the Nazi concentration camps in World War II, and wrote about his experiences and why certain people were able to survive. The survivors had a meaning in their lives—something to live for. Frankl says that we all have freedom, no matter what our circumstances are. We cannot choose the circumstance, but each one of us is free to choose our response to these circumstances. No one can make us feel bad about ourselves. We choose to feel bad as our response. No one can make us angry; we choose to be angry as our response to a situation or person.

I used to let students make me angry. When one would fail to show up for an appointment with me, I would get upset and angry at that student. I would try to phone the student and would become totally preoccupied with that student—or rather by that student's absence. I finally woke up one day and realized I was letting that student totally control my behavior. I decided I would not let that happen any more.

Now when a student is late or fails to show up, I go on about my work as if nothing happened. It's the student's problem, not mine, and the student will have to deal with it. It has made life much more pleasant for me, but I have to confess I am not always successful in being so cool. Sometimes I still get irritated when a student disrupts my schedule, but at least I now recognize the problem—it's me and my response.

Most of us have more control over our lives than we think we do. We like to blame our boss or the system or the infamous "them" instead of taking responsibility for ourselves and our own actions. We need to choose how we respond to the circumstances we find ourselves in.

I have found the idea of "have to" vs. "choose to" a powerful tool in my own life. Here is the analogy. Suppose you have a daughter and her tenth birthday is tomorrow. She is organizing her own birthday party and says, "I'm having a birthday party tomorrow at 4:30 and I'd like you to come."

You reply, "Oh, I'd love to come to your birthday party, but I'm so sorry, I can't. I *have* to go to a meeting."

Now just change one thing. She asks you to come to her party and you answer, "Oh, I'd love to come to your birthday party, but I'm so sorry, I can't. I *choose* to go to a meeting."

When I share this analogy with an audience, there are usually a few gasps in the room. Most of us could never say this. We are so programmed by "have to's" that we don't take responsibility for our own choices.

I think that good leaders intuitively understand the power that freedom of choice gives them. They readily accept responsibility, first for themselves and their own actions, and then for their organizations. They know they must be decisive. Leaders make effective decisions. They also care about the effects of their decisions on other people. They think through the consequences and they act as ethically as they can. Above all they take action and are willing to hold themselves accountable for the results. They choose their responses, and they choose to be responsible.

Ultimately, I think, leadership is a quest for integrity. It starts with the individual leader. You must go deeply inside yourself to discover who you are, your values, and your ethics.

At the same time this quest for integrity involves your relationship with others—especially your followers (or team members). Here the emphasis is on communicating—particularly listening—respecting, caring, inspiring, and building trust.

Finally, the quest for integrity involves the organization or community you serve. It has to do with your vision for the organization and your awareness of the world outside your organization. It has to do with taking the action necessary to accomplish the mission and making sure that the mission and your actions benefit the customers you serve, the people you work with, and the society you live in.

Leadership calls for integrity.

Appendix I

CEOs Interviewed

During the summer of 1995 I interviewed the following CEOs to get their thoughts on what they had found to be most effective in an outside director:

Irving W. Bailey II, Chairman, Providian Corporation
Raymond B. Carey, Jr., retired Chairman, ADT, Inc.
John L. Clendenin, Chairman, BellSouth Corporation
Lyle Everingham, retired Chairman, The Kroger Co.
Roger W. Hale, Chairman, LG&E Energy Corp.
David A. Jones, Chairman, Humana, Inc.
W. Bruce Lunsford, Chairman, Vencor, Inc.
Thomas H. O'Leary, Chairman, Burlington Resources Inc.
John D. Ong, Chairman, BFGoodrich Company
Joseph A. Pichler, Chairman, The Kroger Co.
David M. Roderick, retired Chairman USX Corporation
James D. Woods, Chairman Baker Hughes Incorporated

Appendix II

SYLLABUS
MANAGEMENT 660-LEADERSHIP
BALLARD MORTON, TEACHER

Office: CBPA Building - Room 371
Office hours: Monday-Thursday, 11:00 to 4:00, and by appointment.
Telephone: 852-5612 FAX: 852-7557 E-mail: TBMORT01

This seminar explores leadership from a practical point of view. It is limited to 16 students who interact directly with the teacher, with each other, and with successful leaders.

Students will have the opportunity to develop and practice the skills needed for effective leadership, especially, communicating and interacting with others. We will stress thinking, learning, and creating, and we will focus on the manager and leader as human beings. Students will explore and discuss their own beliefs and values, and they will be encouraged to ask questions and to take responsibility for their own learning.

We will examine and discuss ethics in business — from the viewpoints of the individual and the organization. Students will meet and interact with successful executives from Louisville area organizations.

The objectives of the course are:

1. To give you a better understanding of the manager and leader—what they do and the skills and values they need.
2. To help you become more effective by developing the ability to:
   a. Think critically and creatively;
   b. Communicate clearly;
   c. Interact effectively with others.
3. To improve your skills in communicating—speaking, writing, listening, reading.

4. To give you the chance to interact with and learn from successful leaders (managers, executives).

5. To increase your self-knowledge and self-confidence.

The following books will be required reading (in the order listed):

THE ELEMENTS OF STYLE by Strunk and White
HOW TO GET YOUR POINT ACROSS IN 30 SECONDS
    —OR LESS by Milo Frank
I HEAR YOU by Eastwood Atwater
THE EFFECTIVE EXECUTIVE by Peter Drucker
THE PRINCE by Niccolo Machiavelli
MANAGEMENT AND MACHIAVELLI by Antony Jay
A WHACK ON THE SIDE OF THE HEAD by Roger von
    Oech
THE TAO OF POOH by Benjamin Hoff
LOVE & PROFIT by James A. Autry

Students will also be required to read articles that can be purchased in a special packet from Gray's College Book Store (1915 S. 4th St., 634-1708). We will discuss the main ideas of these books and articles in class, with emphasis on how the students can apply these ideas to their own careers.

A one-page paper—in the form of a business memo—will be required each week. Students will also make oral presentations to the class. We will videotape these presentations to help students improve their speaking skills. Students are required to furnish their own videotape cassette.

Two special projects will take the place of the weekly memo. In one project, each student will prepare a business letter and résumé and then have a private job interview with the teacher. The other will be a team project where students will study a play and then present it to the rest of the class (ANTIGONE, KING LEAR, MACBETH, and OTHELLO).

Students will also work on an informal project. They will

prepare a genogram and a "lifeline." In the genogram they research their own family history, and in the lifeline they draw an autobiographical graph. The object is to gain greater insight into themselves by understanding the patterns and values in their family heritage and in their own lives.

Students will be held accountable for completing all assignments on time. Class attendance is expected. Any absence must be cleared with the teacher in advance.

Two-thirds of the academic grade will be based on written assignments. One-third of the grade will be based on responsiveness in and contribution to the class. Students will have at least five required individual meetings with the teacher. They will frequently be given feedback on how they are doing.

The basic goal in the course is learning—learning how to learn, learning about yourself, and learning what you need to know to lead a fulfilling life.

There will be no exams. *Gaudeamus igitur.*

Note:

The following written materials will be distributed to each student:

1. Explanation of the grading system.
2. Assignment sheets for each class session.

APPENDIX III

Ballard's Bibliophily

TRUMAN by David McCullough

NO ORDINARY TIME by Doris Kearns Goodwin

SMALL IS BEAUTIFUL by E. F. Schumacher

GETTING PAST NO by William Ury

WRITING THE NATURAL WAY by Gabriele Rico

DRAWING ON THE ARTIST WITHIN by Betty Edwards

YOU JUST DON'T UNDERSTAND by Deborah Tannen

MAN'S SEARCH FOR MEANING by Viktor E. Frankl

THE 7 HABITS OF HIGHLY EFFECTIVE PEOPLE by
     Stephen R. Covey

LEADERSHIP IS AN ART by Max DePree

POST-CAPITALIST SOCIETY by Peter F. Drucker

THE HEART AROUSED by David Whyte

THE ENLIGHTENED HEART An Anthology of Sacred Poetry, Edited
     by Stephen Mitchell

ZEN AND THE ART OF MOTORCYCLE MAINTENANCE
     by Robert Pirsig

TAO TE CHING by Lao Tzu (Stephen Mitchell translation)

THE POWER OF MYTH by Joseph Campbell

THE DEATH OF COMMON SENSE by Phillip K. Howard

IN DEFENSE OF ELITISM by William A. Henry

EMOTIONAL INTELLIGENCE by Daniel Goleman

SYNCHRONICITY by Joseph Jaworski

BUSINESS AS A CALLING by Michael Novak

MANAGEMENT OF THE ABSURD by Richard Farson

GODS OF MANAGEMENT by Charles Handy

THE LOYALTY EFFECT by Frederick Reichheld

APPENDIX IV

Some Thoughts On Questions

Always the beautiful answer
who asks a more beautiful question.
—e. e. cummings

Asking questions is the key to learning. The most important intellectual ability humans have yet developed—the art and science of asking questions—is not taught in school.[1]

Through questioning and curiosity we gain knowledge. We discover ourselves and what we need to know. Learning is discovering and growing. We gain new knowledge from new questions—quite often from new questions about old questions.

Once you have learned how to ask questions—relevant and appropriate and substantial questions—you have learned how to learn and no one can keep you from learning whatever you want or need to know.

Our creativity begins with a question. Antony Jay says, "The uncreative mind can spot wrong answers, but it takes the creative mind to spot wrong questions."

The ability to ask the right questions is crucial to leadership. The questions a leader asks send messages about the focus of the organization. Leaders who ask subordinates questions are practicing a sophisticated form of delegation. They cause their subordinates to think for themselves—to develop and grow.

Selecting the right person for a job is one of the important responsibilities of a manager. One of the tools of the selection process is the interview. What makes a good interview? Asking the right questions. (When the role is reversed and you are seeking a job or promotion, you will often gain attention by "asking all the right questions.")

Asking questions is a behavior. If you don't do it, you don't learn it.[1]

It takes courage to ask dumb questions in public. What is a

"dumb" question? Basically it is simple, direct, open-ended and comes from the heart of your curiosity. It's a good idea to keep your questions brief. If you couch your question within an opinionated statement, you put the other person on the defensive. A good, concise question has more chance of eliciting an honest response.[2]

The most important dumb question you can ask is of yourself. Socrates was perhaps the greatest teacher and greatest questioner of all time. His dumb question was basically, "What shall we do and how shall we live?"

I think teachers should spend more time helping students to articulate the urgent questions than demanding right answers.

[1] *Teaching as a Subversive Activity*—Postman & Weingartner
[2] *Creativity in Business*—Ray & Myers

APPENDIX V

GENOGRAM

A genogram is a psychological family tree of the patterns and problems that have been handed down from one generation to another. It identifies the ways in which family members unconsciously project their expectations and wishes onto one another.

1. Grandparents
    Father's
    Mother's
2. Parents
    Father–aunts, uncles
    Mother–aunts, uncles
3. You, brothers, sisters

Looking for patterns of values, decision-making, and relationships. Possible questions to explore:

1. What are their most vivid memories?
2. Background. Where? When? Culture.
3. Career. Why? How?
4. Education. Relative importance?
5. Marriage. When? Where?
6. Values, ideals. What was important? What was stressed?
7. Role of religion.
8. Attitudes. Toward life? Toward children? Toward parents?
9. How did they deal with change? Crisis? Moves? Illness? Divorce? Death?
10. How were family decisions made? Who made them?
11. What was their attitude about money?
12. Interests. Activities. Hobbies. Recreation. Dreams.
13. Who, what influenced them?
14. Health.

15. What was their greatest satisfaction? Accomplishment?
    Disappointment?

Appendix VI

Group Lifeline From *The Human Element* by Will Schutz

Review your role in group situations throughout your lifetime. One of the first things you must know about yourself as a leader is what kinds of roles you are familiar with, which ones you can carry out comfortably and well, which ones you are inexperienced or uncomfortable in, and which ones you probably do not perform very well. You will then be better able to find your place on your team or in your group by continuing what you do best and, as time goes by, strengthening your performance in your weaker roles.

Think about yourself—or better, draw a picture of yourself—as far back as you can remember. Picture yourself at the earliest age you can recall and draw yourself through your lifetime, using the following guidelines:

1. In your family: Where are you in the birth order? What was your role in the family when your parents were home? when they were not at home? when no one was home?

2. With your playmates: Were you a leader? dominant? shy? well liked? ignored? rejected? admired? good at sports? good at school? rebellious? What else?

3. Was your size a factor? your appearance? your abilities or lack of abilities? your gender? your ethnic group? Did you have a nickname?

4. Was there a change in you when the other sex was present? when dating began? Were you popular? unwanted? a loner? a party-goer? sought out? ignored?

Now reflect on how much your present behavior is more understandable in light of these early events.

Think about all your social groups throughout your life—first with people older than you, then with peers, then with people younger or with lower status or position. What roles have you typically played? Which are you good at? poor at? Which do you enjoy? avoid?

How do people typically treat you? In what ways do certain types of people (of a particular age or gender) treat you the same?

How do you expect people to respond to you? What types of reactions do you typically elicit (fatherly, sexual, sisterly, competitive, sympathetic, motherly, helpful, victimized, nasty, critical)?

Given these memories, describe the type of leader you would be in order to make the best use of your strengths and most familiar roles.

As a leader, what would you (initially, at least) want others to take over?

Ballard Morton has been Executive in Residence at the College of Business and Public Administration at the University of Louisville since 1983. He teaches courses that he created in Leadership to graduate students getting their MBA degrees.

He also conducts special programs and courses in leadership development for executives in business and in not-for-profit organizations. In his work with executives he emphasizes effective communications, self-knowledge, ethics, and values.

Before coming to the University of Louisville Mr. Morton was president and chief executive officer of Orion Broadcasting for 16 years. Orion owned a group of television and radio stations and was sold in 1981.

Mr. Morton is a graduate of Yale University. He currently serves on the boards of directors of The Kroger Company, Cincinnati, and LG&E Energy Corp., Louisville. He recently retired from the board of PNC Bank, Kentucky, after serving as a director for 32 years.